Why You Lost That Sale
And What to Do About It!

by

James Yuille

"If you are a salesperson, a sales manager, a professional service provider, a business owner or have any role in a profit-making enterprise and you want better results, this book is a must read."

This book comes with a downloadable workbook filled with exercises to complement the concepts detailed in the book. Go to jamesyuille.com/WYLTSWorkbook to download the workbook prior to reading this book or scan the QR code below. You'll find the corresponding page number of the workbook listed at each relevant section to make it easy for you to find.

Author's note:
For convenience, throughout this book, the terms client and customer; product and service, and male and female are interchangeable.

ISBN: 978-1-7637574-0-0

I'd like to thank all of the people who have employed me over the years to help me develop and refine my skills to the point where I could go out on my own!

REVIEWS

Firstly, thank you for allowing me the privilege of reading and reviewing your book "Why you lost that sale"

This read gave me so many AHA moments!

As a new business owner with limited experience of being a salesperson there were so many moments of "wow, that makes so much sense".

My previous career history in commercial real estate was with a corporate commercial real estate company where I was an office manager and EA to the Director in Charge and have sat in countless sales meetings and marketing meetings where we were provided with sales kits, marketing kits and scripts to follow and although the company is a successful, international company, the message was the same across the board, both nationally and internationally. Cookie cutter approach that the teams were expected to follow.

Your book has given me pause for thought, not only personally but also for my business and what this means for us going forward.

I made many notes and action points in the margins and across the pages!!

- *I have never looked at the properties we market and the products we market and asked myself – if I were the customer, why would I buy this product.. this literally blew my mind and yet seems so simple?*
- *TIPS was a gamechanger!*

- *And also "..Tell me about…." again, so simple but also game changing in my approach to our clients and callers.*
- *FFBC – this now changes the way I look at the properties and services we offer and how I approach marketing these. Utilising the mind map for FFBC will be helpful for me to visualise how to market.*
- *The SWOT analysis/bullet proofing will be essential to our success.*

This book has been an eye opener for me and has reignited my thoughts process about where my business is heading versus where I want it to be.

I will be printing it out and it will become my constant redirection and refer back to "essential item".

Such an easy read too – simple and effective to follow.

Jo Bailey-Green
Principal/Director
Gold Coast Commercial Real Estate

I thoroughly enjoyed reading this book. It's written in an honest unembellished method which allows one to connect with the author and gain a greater understanding of the vast experience and knowledge that James has acquired throughout his personal and professional life.

One of my favourite parts was chapter 5 and the TIPS acronym Trust Identify Propose Set. This little technique is just one of the gems you will find in this book. I would recommend "Why You Lost That Sale And What To Do About It to everyone whether they have been in sales for a long time (like myself) and want to recap or improve their strike rate in sales or for newbies just starting out as it would give them a good foundation to build a very successful career.

James, thank you for all the words of encouragement in the short time we have known each other. You are truly an inspiration to me. Wishing you all the success with the launch and sale of the book. May it be the First in a series.

Lorraine Pearson
Encore Carpet Professionals

I've done a lot of sales training over my business journey thus far. I've heard so much about closing the sale that it really made me sit up and take notice when I read that "You can't close a sale." in James Yuille's book, Why You Lost That Sale: And What To Do About It. Within the pages of this book lie a myriad of golden nuggets that will greatly benefit anyone in the field of sales. I found many of them to be a completely different perspective on traditional sales concepts and to be perfectly honest, it was a refreshing change! If you're looking to up your sales game, I highly recommend starting with this book.

Shari Ware
Effortlessly Organic

CONTENTS

Foreword

How You Lost the Sales and What to Do About It

Building revenue, like any building project, requires expertise.

Revenue forms the foundation for a business and, in the end, is the blood whose absence signals the end of a business.

Sellers stand on the leading edge of revenue and have too often been left poorly enabled.

There are many books dedicated to the art (and science of selling), but few can match the functionality of James' wonderful book.

In 1986, James and I were awarded a trip to Japan as our employers' leading sellers. James was always highly motivated, succinct, and action oriented. His selling ability manifested into stellar results even then.

Having my own sales capability practice, I became engaged with an organisation in late 2015 quite serendipitously. The group had signed a global contract, and my training was to cover the Australia and New Zealand teams. The leader of this team was enthusiastic when others who were asked to follow a global rollout might be inclined to resist or go through the motions. This leader embraced the prospect of introducing sales processes and discipline within a highly competitive market.

"I have always been an advocate of sales training. I credit sales training with being an integral part of my own personal success," said my new client sponsor in late 2015.

"Oh, that is good to hear", I replied, feeling grateful to be working with a leader who would be prepared to drive the new discipline necessary to achieve the improvement dividends.

"Tell me more about your own experiences," I asked, not realising I was using one of the absolute gems offered in this book.

"I had the good fortune to work with a sales trainer who recognised that I was a visual thinker. I needed to ask my prospects questions that solicited a response that I could more easily understand and quickly integrate," said this sales leader.

"Really? I would love to know who it was," I enquired with curiosity and a little discomfort that I might not be as credible as I hoped.

"James Yuille", David Newington replied.

I can state with great assurance and confidence, based on my direct experience, that James delivers results. All those who choose to embark on the reading journey here will gain insight into what you can do to create these results for yourself and/or your sales team.

Selling has never been more challenging, and Marketing has never been more mysteriously expensive. James's book equips you to meet and take on the sales challenge and to direct your marketing dollars wisely.

To take a quote used within this book:

'What you are speaks so loudly I can't hear what you are saying'.

If you care about building your business.

If you care about others investing in your business.

Learn about selling.

Learn with this book.

Make your mark.

Murray Grimston
Director
Focus Right Training and Coaching

Introduction

Every business owner, every sales manager, and every salesperson has asked or has been asked these questions many times. "How do we increase sales?" "How can we grow the business?'

The drive to increase sales to generate more revenue is the core activity of every business. Unless you're making sales, your business will slowly fade away.

Sales are what makes you money. Everything else is an expense that erodes your profits, and decreasing expenditure is difficult.

What is surprising, and what the author has witnessed throughout his career, is that very few companies have documented sales processes. Neither do their owners, sales managers, or salespeople have any sales training behind them.

This begs a serious question: Why trust the task of making and increasing sales, the most important role in the company, to people with no training and no process to follow?

You wouldn't seek legal or accounting advice from someone without a degree. You wouldn't let an unlicensed electrician or plumber work on your property.

Even more concerning, most businesses don't know the key numbers around their sales efforts.

Ask them how many leads they generate in a typical month; they don't know. Ask how much each lead costs or where it came from; again, they won't know.

Ask about their conversion rate, the average sale value, or the lifetime value of a client, and you will likely be met with a glazed look and a vague answer.

The core task of sales management is to know these numbers. The only sales management task that is more important is to instil a proven, replicable, accountable sales process to their sales team.

Those responsible for managing sales often focus on the wrong things. The typical focus is on lead generation, answering objections and sales closing techniques.

This book looks at the entire sales process, from advertising and lead generation to accepting the customer's request to purchase. It provides a simple, proven system that empowers everyone involved to know what to say (and what NOT to say) and a review process to check what went wrong if the sale is lost. It is really a DIY sales coaching system in written form.

Hence the title, "Why You Lost That Sale: And What To Do About It".

If you're a business owner, a sales or business development manager, a sales person or even a receptionist, this book is a "must read".

Here's what you will learn in this book:

Scripts Are Just a Guide
Why strictly sticking to the script can destroy your chances of making the sale.

Let's Get Started
Some fundamental principles.

How a University Drop-Out Generated Multi-Millions of Dollars in Sales and Profits
I had to make it work, and my boss couldn't help me.

How to Develop a Successful Business Mindset
Sales isn't a game; you're playing for keeps.

The TIPS Process and How to Make It Work for You
A proven framework for making sales at any level.

How to Find Out Quickly What They Want to Buy
Discover the strategy behind the "Tell me about" question.

How to Make Your Proposal Sound Like Music to Their Ears
When they say "Ah ha, that's interesting", you're on the right track.

Questions You Must Answer Before You Move Forward
A series of simple questions that anyone in sales should be asking themselves before attempting to sell their product.

How to Find Prospects
From cold calling to loyalty programs – there's more than one way to find prospects.

Consultative Selling
Your job is not to sell to your prospects; you are there to remove

pain, solve problems, or present opportunities.

Why People Buy, and Why They Don't
Find out why someone didn't buy from you and what to do about it.

What to Do Now the Sale Is Made
Why keeping clients is as important as finding them.

How to Avoid Being the Next Marketing Victim
Popular marketing concepts debunked!

How to Use the Power of Others to Your Advantage
Learn why referral business is so valuable and how to get it in spades.

How To Impress Anyone Inside 60 Seconds
Because we know that first impressions count.

How to Deliver Awesome Customer Service
Customer service is not just the salesperson's responsibility: it's everyone's!

The Eight Deadly Sales Sins – What They Are and How to Avoid Them
Learn the eight unforgivable sales sins so you don't make them yourself.

How to Increase Your Personal Effectiveness
How much time will you waste today?

Chapter 1
Scripts Are Just a Guide

In the early 1990's I was investigating the purchase of a franchise. I wanted something structured, with systems, effective marketing, and a known brand. Retail, especially food, didn't cut it. And most service or outward-bound franchises had negligible lead-generation processes.

A security business triggered my attention. After three lengthy meetings, the principals invited me to visit one of their franchises and work inside it for three days.

I was flown from Brisbane to Adelaide where I spent a day in the office listening to the telemarketers make calls and book appointments. Late that afternoon, I accompanied Rex, a very enthusiastic young salesman, as he conducted his appointments.

Hearing the sales script at the first appointment, I grimaced. No sale resulted from that visit and as we drove away, he called the office to make a report and obtain his next assignation.

Ten minutes later, he delivered his rote-pitch, and again, no sale ensued. The discomfort as he phoned base was patent. He was clearly under pressure. They had an expectation of a sale, per person, per day. This was Wednesday and he had only made one for the week.

As we arrived at the next appointment, I asked him if it would be ok if I became involved in the conversation. He was unsure, not wanting to deviate from the script. When I suggested that my mere presence alone may have contributed to his nervousness and I wanted to help him make a sale, he agreed

The couple we were visiting were in their late 50's. Rex began again and after ten minutes it was apparent that he was flailing. They weren't buying. An idea came to me. "Rex, let's just pop out to the car to get a system to show them." He looked at me with daggers in his eyes. Rex needed the voice of authority. "Come on, let's go"

Outside, I offered a suggestion...I'll tell you more about that later...

Chapter 2

Let's Get Started

You've got a problem and need a solution, so let's cut straight to the chase...

You're reading this book because you want to find an easier way to generate more business.

If you're like most people, you've wondered exactly what it is that makes the best salespeople and the best businesses successful month after month, year after year. It seems like you're doing the same things: advertising, seeing prospects, following up leads and meetings, yet the other guy still gets better results.

Why? What is it that makes some people more successful at sales and marketing than others?

What do they know that you don't? Well, you can discover the answers to that question right here. Then all you'll have to do is apply them...And that's the first secret of attaining the heights of success – you must do something different!

This is not an instant fix. Nor is it a simple overnight read that will reap results from tomorrow. It's not a short course in selling.

You may think that some of the things you'll find here are too basic. You may even think that those basics can't make too much difference. Maybe, but everyone needs to get back to fundamentals from time-to-time. If you play or watch competitive sports, you'll know that at the beginning of the season, every team gets back to basics. You cannot progress to higher levels if you ignore them.

What you will find as you take the time to read, study and apply the concepts and processes discussed, is that it will make a difference. Your access to higher performance is right here, right now.

This information has helped everyone, from raw beginners to seasoned professionals, improve their performance and results, and become your companion, just as it became for my very first client, David Newington.

David and I worked together for several weeks; he was running a fledgling software company that his mother and stepfather had helped him start. His mother had recognised that despite his degree in marketing, David was struggling and needed help. The initial contact was made with a marketing consultant friend of mine to whom she went for advice. The consultant and I had been mates for years and I had been telling him that I was going to write a sales training manual—one day.

Recognising that David's issue was that David couldn't sell, he called and said he had a client for me and was the manual ready? Over two weekends I wrote the original manuscript and went to work with David. The results were spectacular. Sales started to happen and within a year, the venture had become profitable. David's stepfather bought the business back from him. David entered a new career in the travel industry where he soared through the ranks to become a senior sales executive in the company's Los Angeles office.

In 2005 I was in LA and caught up with David. Proudly, he showed me the battered, dog-eared manual I had provided him all those years ago. The pages were covered with hand-written notes.

Many bore coffee stains and it was falling apart. I sent him a new one and he bought two others, one for his state sales manager, the other for the national sales manager.

This book is not just something you browse, consign to a dark corner, or read through once and discard the information contained thereafter. You take it to work, refer to it before appointments, and afterwards compare your techniques and methods with those it espouses. It's the re-vitaliser, the complacency checker.

It took 33 years to write the first edition. No, I'm not a slow scribe; rather, the information, knowledge and research therein are derived from a career focused on but one result – finding and keeping customers. The principles and processes are proven, have universal application and they work.

Before we move on, here are my definitions of common sales and marketing terms used throughout this book:

The Gain and Retain More Customers Sales and Marketing Dictionary
"Marketing" – One-way communication about a product or service a purpose of which is to encourage recipients of the communication to enquire about, purchase or use the product or service.

"Selling" – Two-way communication about a product or service a purpose of which is to encourage recipients of the communication to purchase or use the product or service.

"Profit Point" – That point when the buyer agrees to your proposal. Your challenge is to increase the number of "profit points" you have in a week, a day, an hour...

"Sale" – The mutually agreeable exchange of goods or services for money.

"Commercial Insanity" – Investing time, money and effort into a product or service without first establishing that a market exists for it.

"Marketing Insanity" – Investing thousands in image and branding, and in repeating ads and sales letters that don't work.

Chapter 3

How a University Drop-Out Generated Multi-Millions of Dollars in Sales and Profits

Even knowing that, most of us continue doing what we've always done and get what we always have. We go on making the same mistakes and wonder why nothing changes.

So how do you know that the way you are doing something is the best method of doing it? Did you just stumble on it? We tend to get so caught up doing things in a fashion that we never stop to look for a better way.

But simple changes can have profound results.

Something as simple as changing the way you answer the phone can have a huge impact. It did with one client who changed the way he handled incoming enquiry calls, and that alteration increased the number of face-to-face sales opportunities by 320%.

Nevertheless, whether by blind faith or sheer ignorance, people still do what they've always done; usually what their industry considers to be standard practice and then wonder why they don't make headway, why their business doesn't thrive, and why it ends up being just another commodity.

They are working with flawed concepts, techniques, and processes.
Selling is like that. Sales people still struggle to make quota, led by business owners and managers who, in turn, either learned flawed

techniques themselves, or learned through some form of magical osmosis. **These flaws are perpetuated.**

Flawed concepts like, "It's a numbers game", "Close the sale", "We have to get the name out there" and, "Advertising for exposure" echo mindlessly through business houses today, just as they did 30 years ago.

If you think I'm being a little hard or even cynical, you're right. Very few people in sales take it as rolled-gold advice to continually educate themselves. Many have never had any formal training whatsoever.

It's interesting that people who should know, people with impeccable credentials in business success – people like Robert Kiyosaki and Jay Abraham – consistently advocate that learning the craft of professional consultancy selling is one of, if not, the most important skill you need for business success.

Jay Abraham made the statement that, "The quickest, easiest way to improve the performance of a business is to invest in consultative sales training". ("Power to Profit" seminar, Los Angeles, May 2005)

When I ask clients or seminar attendees how many books on sales and marketing they've read in the last one, two or five years, it's disappointing to find that in most instances, you can count the numbers on one hand.

Why is it that businesses both big and small continue to rely on untrained employees to perform the most vital task – revenue generation? You wouldn't hire an untrained accountant, a first-year apprentice electrician, an articled law clerk or a jerry-builder, would you? So why rely on untrained salespeople?

I suppose some of the blame for absence of training and the lack of self-education is historical.

Years ago, your employment as a salesperson was based on one or two simple criteria: if you fogged up the mirror by breathing on it and could talk with your head submerged in cement, you would be hired.

You got the job because you showed up for the interview. Don't laugh; I've seen this more than once. Would you hire a financial controller or CEO that way? No, and neither should you so engage a salesperson either.

Another failure point is when your knowledge of the process of an industry is used as the key selection criteria.

That you understand mortgages is seen as an appropriate qualification to work as a mortgage broker. Or your knowledge of welding qualifies you to sell welding gear. Certainly, both are relevant, but given the addition of good sales training, the results will be significantly better.

Selling was once regarded as an activity that required participants to talk incessantly. It was also commonly believed that you had to be able to close the sale, using one of a series of manipulative questioning techniques that would somehow conjure the customer's agreement to buy from you.

That technique is called, "Show and Sell" and you can still see it used in shopping centres and at markets by a variety of merchants.

In the business world, the day of the snake-oil salesperson has passed. The Internet has changed the way we buy. Consumers are more informed than at any other time in history.

Today's salespersons must be professionals. They must build a relationship with the customer.

The level of skill required today far surpasses the old snake-oil honchos. The level of determination and tenacity hasn't changed though. Success still requires salespeople to contact strangers, make phone calls, drive in the rain, and get knock-backs from buyers. Those things will never change.

Selling isn't a thing you can do successfully whilst waiting for something else to come along. Just as you can't simply try NASCAR racing, you can't try selling. There's a learning curve. As Ross Bischoff a twenty-year plus Real Estate Professional says, "You don't just try selling – selling tries you."

If you think that selling is an easy way to make a living; that people will queue all day to buy from you; that all you have to do is show up and your budget is realised, then you're sadly misguided and probably looking at the wrong job.

By good fortune I learned this lesson a long time ago. Let me outline two key learning experiences…

My sales career started in Adelaide at the ripe old age of 21. I had been studying economics at University and was bored legless. They were teaching me to be a public servant and I didn't want to be one. Always a bit of a rebel, I was really a hippie back then and the thought of being sentenced to public service mundanity was, well, unthinkable.

I quit University and laboured on a farm for a year. I wanted to get fit while I worked out what to do with my life.

Somewhere along the way, I picked up a copy of Napoleon Hill's, Think and Grow Rich and by book's end, had decided that a career in sales sounded good. It had the twin appeals of freedom and money, both exciting to a 21-year old with few ties.

An ad in the *Adelaide Advertiser* for a sales trainee offered entry into the then fledgling telecommunications industry. It asked for written applications, so, using one of the ideas I'd read in Hill's book, I wrote an application that said I'd work for a month without obligation to them.

The offer was if they didn't like me or felt I wasn't up to it; they could dispense with my services and they'd owe me nothing. If I showed promise, if they thought I was trainable and could produce a result, they would pay me for the month, and I'd join their team.

After starting in the job, I found out that my application letter had so blown them away that they didn't interview anyone else. The ensuing interviews were mere formalities.

My first direct-mail piece had delivered a 100% conversion rate.

Not only that, but without recognising it, I'd effectively used a risk-reversal strategy. I'd identified their biggest risk in hiring me, what they could do if I were no good and eliminated it by my offer to work for free.

So, I started the job, eager, enthusiastic - and **naive.**

My training taught me to sell intercom phone systems and Bundy clocks (those machines where you punch in a card to tell the Boss what time you clocked on and off every day) by means of a printed storybook.

I gathered prospects by walking the streets and door-knocking business houses with this simple question:

"I'm updating a mailing list and I'd appreciate if you could tell me the name of the person who buys office equipment here, please"

In twelve months, I physically cold-called every business house in Adelaide.

Then I'd phone the business and ask for an appointment to see the buyer. Back then, making the appointment was easier than it is now but even so, my conversion rate was only about 1 appointment from 15-20 calls.

Once at the meeting, I'd show the prospect through the book and then move to the 'close' which was, "What do you think?" *(Yes, that was the scripted line...)*

Invariably, the answer was, "We'll think about it"

My pro-activity over the first 30-days was enough for me to keep the job but it was becoming painfully apparent that the methodology they had provided wasn't going to work for me. I had a high-maintenance girlfriend and a big car payment to make.

There had to be a better way...

I closeted myself in the bedroom one weekend and asked a simple question that changed my destiny. Here it is...

"If I were the customer, why would I buy this product?"

I had to think as my customer thought. As eminent copywriter and marketer Joe Vitale says, "You have to get out of your ego and into theirs"

Understand, I was a Uni dropout, had been on a farm for twelve months driving a tractor, building fences, and herding cows. I lived and worked all day on a remote property with the farm manager and his wife and two sons.

I had had almost no contact with the outside world, let alone with the middle-aged business boffins to whom I was trying to sell. They were foreigners to me.

Yet there I was, fitted out in a suit and tie, trying to convince them to buy this (then) state-of-the-art technology. And they weren't wearing it. At that point, my future was on the line. Something had to change, and over that weekend, it did.

I inadvertently discovered the concept of benefits. I unlocked the puzzle by writing down a list of everything those machines did and what that meant to the buyer.

The following Monday, I re-booted my strategy. With invigorated gravitas, I sourced prospects offering new messages like, "Mr Prospect, if I could show you how to make your phone communications more efficient, would you allow me 20 minutes to explain how to do it?"

They started to say, "Yes" in large numbers.

Now I had to work out what to do next. Here's what happened…

When I sat down in the meeting, I'd engage in the usual small talk and then say, "Mr Prospect, does this situation (painting a likely communication error) ever occur here?"

Invariably, he'd say that it did. I'd then ask about the degree of inconvenience it caused, and if it looked like I could sell the machines, I explained how my solution would help alleviate the inconvenience.

Sales went through the roof.

That year, as the youngest, most inexperienced salesperson in the whole company, I topped the sales figures.

Seasoned professionals in Australia's largest cities were left behind.

It was as if I'd found the Holy Grail.

This success carried on for several years, and eventually I found myself in Sydney selling telephone answering machines. They were expensive then – the top of the range machine costing over $1200 at a time when a new car could be purchased for around $3,000.

Our target market was trades people – plumbers, carpenters, and the like.

I designed a promotional campaign that ran in the then afternoon newspapers. The headline was simple and very effective. It said:

How to Answer Every Customer Call – Even When You're Not Home.

I would get the enquiry calls from the adverts, fix a time to go see them, load the car with new machines and spend my evenings visiting people in their homes.

I was a little lazy, I guess. The machines were heavy, so I'd leave them in the car and go into the house with just my diary doubling as my notebook. They would ask me where the machine was.

I would answer by saying that we had three different models and as I didn't know which would suit. I added that I'd thought they wouldn't have wanted me to carry three machines into their home. True, they didn't.

Then I asked this killer question. It made me thousands of dollars in commissions…

"Why do you think you need an answering machine?"

They would proceed to tell me. They talked about the problems their wife faced because she daren't leave the home, even to collect the kids from school or go to the bank, in case they missed a call. I'd ask how having a machine to answer the phone would change their routines; what flexibility it would provide, and how long they would be away from the house if they could be.

*(**Sidebar:** this line of questioning is intended to have them tell me why they needed my product.)*

From the answers they gave me, I would explain how the machine would solve the problem for them, and then I'd recommend a suitable model, discuss how much it was and ask them if they would like to see one.

The answer was always, "Yes". I'd get a new one from the car, plug it into their phone line, record a message on it and then ask them to have the neighbour or a friend ring them back.

The call would come in; the caller would hear a message asking them to leave a message and they would do so. (It sounds simple today doesn't it, but back then, these machines were hi-tech!)

The result was a sale almost every time. In fact, I rarely had to unplug the machine and put it back in the car. If I had gone out with four machines in the car, I would never return with more than one.

My peers couldn't understand how I did it. They would go into their appointments lugging equipment and show off every button and feature.

Invariably, the voice said, "Thank you, we'll let you know" and back to the office they'd toddle next morning with their stock of machines intact and very crestfallen.

I never really thought about it much either. I didn't know how my technique differed from that of my peers. One day our Sales Manager, Colin Smith, asked us each to do a role-play presentation of our sales call.

I did the shortest product demonstration of anyone in the group. They laughed at its brevity. I relished pointing to my name at the top of the sales figures where it had resided for months.

Afterwards Colin said to me quietly, "Just keep on doing what you're doing. The others might get the message one day."

As I began to study the business of selling, I realised that my ongoing success was because I had developed the ability to ask the right questions, listen for the answer and then move on to the next phase of the sale. It just seemed the natural thing to do.

My reasoning was that I couldn't get anyone to buy anything they didn't want or need. All I had to do, I figured, was to make them aware that they had a need, that a solution was easy, and that the solution was worth the money they were spending.

It hasn't changed. I still adopt the same techniques I used all those years ago. Along the way, I've used them to successfully sell many different products and services.

What are the best questions you could ask your potential customers? Do you think that having them answer the questions would help them realise how great your service is?

The process comprises four key steps, which I refer to as TIPS. The TIPS process is explained in detail in Chapter 5.

There are some important concepts you need to grasp to use the TIPS process effectively.

Businesses that demonstrate continued success have a cultural mindset that focuses on two things:

1. That sales and marketing are the drivers of the business
2. That the focus must be on the customer

That mindset is explained in the next chapter.

Remember

Constantly perform reality checks on your product/service by asking this question:

"If I were the customer, would I buy this, and why?"

There is an exercise on Page 4 of the downloadable workbook (jamesyuille.com/WYLTSWorkbook) to help you with this.

People buy from you, not necessarily because they understand what you do, but because they feel understood and they believe that your product is of benefit to them because you helped them identify that for themselves.

Chapter 4

How to Develop a Successful Business Mindset

Most business owners I've encountered enjoy a love affair with their product.

They started because they liked plumbing but wanted to be a bookkeeper or a HR consultant. So, they open a business to do that and then find they need customers to survive.

The battle begins; How to find and keep customers.

I hear prolific stories and meet many people in businesses who say they just want to do graphic art, paint houses or whatever. They all say the same thing, "I don't want to sell, I just want to make/do/be..."

If that's how you think, let me prevent years of pain and anguish; let me save you thousands of dollars and maybe even your home and your family. Don't go into business. Stay in your job, or if the job itself is the problem, change jobs.

You might be the best printer in town, you might be the finest chef, you might have the nicest function rooms but if you can't generate clients, there is no point.

Here's the harsh reality: Unless you can sell your service, you're unemployed!

Building a better mousetrap is only part of the battle. You must be able to sell it. Better to be a brilliant marketer with an OK product than a hopeless marketer with a brilliant product.

If you're not yet in business, and are thinking about buying or starting a business, you would do well to start by identifying a market with which you're comfortable and find something they need that you can sell to them. Unless you're certain there's a demand for what you've got, no matter how good you think it is, you'll find it hard to sell. There's no point being a hungry dog following an empty meat-truck.

In other words, if nobody is going to buy your product, you're not going to make any money so quitting before you go too far would be the smartest thing to do.

Better still, be a brilliant marketer with a product that fills a slot in a hungry market! We both know it's not even essential to have the best product. I'm sure you can think of markets where the best-selling product isn't the best, for example, Yellow Pages, hamburgers, fried chicken and energy drinks. How do you think those products became the best-selling ones?

Doing what you do is the result - the payoff - for generating a client. It stands to reason then, that if you want to do more of what you do, and eat, clothe your family and keep the roof over your head, you must get better at selling it.

Understand that the profit is made at the time the client agrees to your proposition. I call this moment "The Profit Point". It's the moment when your buyer says, "Yes" to your proposition. The events leading up to that point are your investment in marketing and sales, and everything after that is an expense.

Profound? I think so.

Pause and consider what you just read. Marketing and sales are an investment; delivery and fulfilment are expenses. A vastly different proposition to the conventional business theory, isn't it?

The purpose of a business is to make money for the owner. It does that by, first, staying in business. That's not as easy as it sounds. Statistics show that significant small businesses fail to earn their owners even a subsistence living.

Most small businesses fail on account of the owner's inability to get out of the "doing" because the owner doesn't understand marketing, leverage (getting others to do the work), systems (making sure it's done right every time) and the need to make a profit.

If you're slaving away at your business, working all hours of the day, night, and weekend, drawing less than you're paying your staff, what's the point? And don't ever think you're going to be able to sell it. Who's going to buy your sinking ship?

When you look at the point of agreement to do business as the point of profit, you can then see why marketing and sales are investments.

It follows then, that to make more profit, you must either generate more sales or make sales that are more profitable.

When you apply a scientific approach to marketing, when you test and measure everything to the point of refinement, you can then adjust your results by simply adjusting your marketing efforts.

If you *know* that every time you invest $1,000 into a tested marketing process and it produces a $7,500 return, when you want more business, just spend another $1,000. It will generate roughly the same return.

Marketing and innovation are now your clear choice focus points. The delivery of product or provision of service is where you need to be efficient. Delegate, sub-contract, outsource; do whatever you can to make this aspect of your business efficient. Spend your time on marketing and the innovation of new methods to solve your client's problems.

Business is all about getting and keeping clients. It involves sales and marketing. When you get this right, your business is successful, and you prosper. If you don't like that, then being in business is not for you.

Recently I was invited to speak to the swimming pool industry body about advertising online. Several members wanted to know more, including a guy whose business was floundering. He wasn't sure if he should keep the doors open. He had a young family to feed; his wife was pregnant again and the opportunity to become someone else's employee was very attractive.

His overheads were low; he had what I saw to be a unique selling proposition in a very competitive market and a reasonable website that had been built as an online brochure instead of for generating enquiries. He had been reliant on referrals to grow his business and just wasn't getting enough leads.

He's a decent guy. I asked him if he would be prepared to put $1,500 on the desk to do some online advertising and to make small tweaks to his website. On that basis, we did some research, added some stunning photos of his work to the site, changed the copy to be more customer-focused and added a call-to-action on each page.

Within days of launching the new campaign, things started to turn around. Within three months his book was full of work and in November, we had to pause his advertising as he simply couldn't cope with any more orders. We resumed the campaign after

Christmas and I cheekily asked him if working for someone else was still on his radar? The response was emphatic; "No way!"

To quote Jay Abraham:

"You are always a sales and marketing company. Your greatest leverage isn't operational or managerial. It's marketing. Marketing is the only thing that can give you leverage. Marketing is the vehicle that gives you distinction. It is the only thing that stops you becoming a commodity."

As we said right back at the beginning, the focus of your business must be on the customer. Customers provide sales, cash flow and profits.

Getting clients comes down to identifying what you have to offer them and then packaging your advertising, marketing, and presentations to meet that need. You are essentially a problem solver. The problem you must solve is the gap between where your clients are and where they want to be, or what they don't have and want, and where your product bridges that gap.

When you ask astute questions and listen attentively to their answers, you find out what issues customers are concerned about.

What are astute questions?

They are the ones that help you identify what's going on in their business or in their lives. They're the questions that uncover their challenges and how you can provide them with pleasure or help them avoid pain.

These are the simple motivators for all decisions: the gaining of pleasure or avoidance of pain. In business, most people often hear this expressed as, 'making or saving money'. When you think about it, both expressions mean the same thing. It's worth noting that most respond to the pain of losing money ten times faster than they do to the pleasure of having more money to spend.

OK, so there will be more complex theories expressed about buying motivation: fear, hope, reward, saving face and more. The bottom line is that decisions are made based on avoiding pain or gaining pleasure.

It is vital to understand the benefit of whatever you sell. Your entire reason for existence is the value you can bring to your customer. When they ask, "What's in it for me?" that's when you provide them with value.

Remember that all along, your customers are asking, *"What's in this for me?"*

To answer that, answer the question I asked myself all those years ago…

"If I were the customer, why would I buy this product?"

Many businesses and salespeople struggle to make their monthly targets/budgets. As a result, they're fragile financially. For them, life is a matter of trying not to exhaust their liquidity before they run out of month. Their long-term planning consists of how to meet next month's rent or the impending phone bill. Five and ten-year plans and goals simply don't exist.

If I asked you to email me a copy of either your personal goals for the next five years, or a copy of your business plan if you own a business, would you be able to?

Over 90% of people couldn't. Yet without exception, every book ever written about making it big personally or financially states that the key to success in any venture is to have a detailed, documented plan or goal sheet. Hundreds of speakers and trainers throughout the world make good livings spreading this message, yet most people fail to heed it.

The mere act of writing down your plans increases the chance of them actually happening by as much as 75%.

I'm going to ask you to make some plans and to ask you to plan two hours every week for the next few weeks to work on your sales process.

Here's a challenge; get serious about what you do and focus on future success.

You need to discipline yourself to change some habits and practices you currently employ in your daily business activities.

When I'm requested to assist a salesperson who is looking to achieve better results, the first thing I ask is; 'with what does he or she want help?' Most require a "quick fix" to cure what they perceive to be their biggest problem.

The most requested "quick fix" is an easy way to, "close the sale".

Would that interest you—an easy way to close the sale?

Most salespeople are looking for a set of magic words that will make every prospect buy. It is very uncommon for someone to ask how to get the prospect / buyer / customer / client to talk about their problems and about how they, the salesperson can help them.

I dislike the term, "close the sale". I'd like to find the person who first coined it and wash their mouth out! It's a degrading, unprofessional term and one you really must eliminate from your lexicon. Along with any other cliché from a 1960's hard selling manual. You are a professional, one who doesn't use terms like, "close the sale".

The concept comes from the Wild West where itinerant peddlers would ride the stagecoach or train from town-to-town. In each location they would aggressively peddle their wares from a soapbox, providing instant cures for a variety of ailments.

Cash in hand, they bedded down at the saloon and took the first coach out the following day to avoid being lynched by their recently fleeced customers. They had to close sales every day simply to afford room and board and the next onward fare.

That's an unhealthy and unwise business model to follow…

Suffice it to say that techniques like, "Tie Downs" and, "Circle Closes" are well past their use-by date. Today's customers are better informed about you, your product, and your company than ever before. Relationships equal money (R=M). Build a relationship, open the sale, and allow the customer to cross the line, say, "Yes" and, they close the sale for you.

That *you* can't close a sale, flies in the face of all previous sales training wisdom. Yet there have been studies done that categorically prove the customer closes the sale, the salesperson opens the opportunity for the sale to occur.

In 1981, an Australian, Dr Michael Hewitt-Gleeson, undertook the study. It is discussed in his book, *The X10 memeplex* (published by Pearson Education Australia). I recommend that you read it. Dr Hewitt-Gleeson has challenged several major names in sales training to prove him wrong. None has accepted the challenge.

The concept of, 'closing the sale' is redundant.

You simply cannot close a sale. All you can do is open it. Your customers will always make the decision for themselves, always.

When you eliminate the term, "Close the sale" from your vocabulary and look instead to opening a problem-solving relationship with your client, the picture, and the result changes for the better.

There are several words and phrases that can, without you knowing it, lose you the sale. Two words I recommend you eliminate as soon as possible are, "appointment" and, "quote". Appointments are made with people who you fear might cause you pain, e.g. proctologists and dentists. *(With apologies to both professions.)*

It is much better to organise a time to, "drop around" or a time to, "get together". It's friendly, congenial, something you might say to a friend.

"Quote" is similar because we've all been drilled that when you get a quote, you should get three. So, if you say you're coming to give a quote, you're likely to find yourself in competition with at least two other people.

The other thing about quotes is that we tend to look to the cheapest. And, unless you're positioned to be the cheapest, this isn't a game you want to play.

Instead, you're better to give them a schedule of what's involved, or an authority to install or proceed. You want to make sure you're not in the business of doing quotes. You're in the business of selling the product or service for which you're quoting. Why do we offer "free quotes?" Why not charge and rebate if the project goes ahead? I know why: because everyone else in your industry does free quotes.

Dan Kennedy asks the question, "Do you want to be in the business of doing free quotes or in the business of making money?" Be bold, be brave; start charging to do quotes. If nothing else, it eliminates those who are, "just looking".

A colleague had a builder client who decided he'd had enough of hard work and looked for a better way to make money. He recognised that hundreds of home handymen wanted to do relatively small backyard projects themselves however didn't know exactly how. He ran adverts in the local newspapers promoting that for a modest fee, he would come out to explain how to do jobs like building retaining walls or laying concrete slabs for sheds.

He would do a sketch and list the materials they would need to get the job done and leave with his fee. Easy money! But wait, there's more... He also worked out how much it would cost the family if he were to do the job and he kept that quiet.

After four or five weeks he would casually revisit them to see how the job was going. Invariably it wasn't! Frequently there was a pile of materials in the yard waiting to be used.

What happened next was pure poetry. He'd simply say, "Would you like me to get it done for you? It will be about $600."

Close to half said, "Yeah, great, get it done please."

Money for jam and what's more, he subcontracted everything. See how he avoided doing free quotes and eliminated any competition? What's more, he rarely had to buy materials. It's a simple, replicable and profitable business model that could easily be franchised.

A client of mine is in the home improvement industry selling amongst other things, insect screens and doors. I taught him a line that worked sensationally...

Callers would invariably ask him for a price over the phone. He replied that he couldn't give an accurate figure as there were too many variables. His intent was to be invited to the house so he could talk directly with the homeowner.

Conscious that he wasn't the cheapest supplier, he used this line; "I suggest the job will be in the region of $400 - $480 and I'm happy to come out to measure up to give you an accurate figure. Is that price range ok; I'm never going to be the cheapest in town so if you're buying only on price, please tell me as it won't be worth coming out."

He was rarely refused, and his conversion rate went from two or three appointments and from ten enquiries to around seven. Sales significantly increased and over the next 18 months his revenue quadrupled. What's more, he never lost a job for not being the cheapest.

The lesson here is that he took price out of the equation and I'll refer to this in detail later.

Selling can be compared to a sporting event: baseball, basketball, football; it doesn't matter. In any sport, if your team falls too far behind on the scoreboard, it gets hard to pull back the deficit. Being one hundred and fifty runs behind in the second innings with one wicket in hand, or 20 points down with four minutes to play is tough.

When you get into situations like this in a sporting event, it's fair to say you didn't start well. The sales process is the same in that trying to close the sale puts you at the equivalent level of risk. It's dangerous.

You can't close a sale and you must not waste time trying. **You can only open a sale.** That's where the time and energy should be spent. Remember this: more sales are lost right here than at any other time in the process!

Selling is about relationships. It's about creating and sustaining relationships, not asking a series of questions each phrased to give a, "yes" answer with the last question in the series being, "Do you want to buy?"

To become proficient at anything, you should first take stock of where you are when you start and have a goal of where you'd like to be. Here's a checklist to help you work out where your sales skill level might be right now. Once you have figured out which stage you are at, then you can plot a path to where you want to be, and when.

Unconscious incompetence
You don't know that you don't know what you're doing.

This is most likely how you were when you started in your first sales job. Keen, enthusiastic, and wet behind the ears!

You went at it like a raging bull, demo materials in one hand, order forms in the other, giving your pitch to anyone who breathed. (Pitch - there's a phrase I hate!
Use *presentation or consultation* if you must describe the process of talking about your product.)

Maybe you got some sales by chance and wondered how you did it. This is really an unsustainable state in which to be, especially if you're asked a tricky question.

It also tends to be short-lived, as the income resulting from this level of competence is very low and won't sustain you.

Conscious incompetence

You suddenly realise that you don't know what you're doing. (This is when most people who quit sales, quit.)

The realisation comes when faced with a series of tricky or embarrassing questions over which you fumble.

This is when an experienced buyer realises that you're new and, regrettably for you, decides to poke some fun at your expense.

Often you will run backwards and forwards between the buyer and your office getting answers to more and more trivial questions.

One day you realise the customer's not going to buy after all and you've been had.

Buyers like this do exist and before long, you'll meet one. I hope you will turn the experience to your advantage and grow as a result.

Conscious competence

When you think you know what you're doing but still need to think about it.

You are beginning to understand when things are going well (or badly) with a buyer.

You are able now to visit larger buyers with confidence, but every now and again, feel a little overawed.

You still need help with some calls from either your manager or your supplier.

Unconscious competence
When you're so good at what you're doing, that you don't even have to think about it.

When the right words come out every time.

When everything clicks into place.

When your sales go through the roof.

A word of warning about unconscious competence...
At this stage, the unconscious competent salesperson stops growing, stops learning and stops studying. He or she becomes complacent and starts to miss opportunities. Never think you know it all. A true professional in *any* field continues to study!

I still attend seminars, read books, watch webinars. Even if I only learn one thing, it hones my skills and keeps me interested, learning, and growing.

Get the message here:

Your ability to continue to make a good living depends upon your knack of staying with the game. No pro sports player goes into a match without training and practice.

No Doctor or Dentist lets a year pass without reading about new techniques and the latest treatments; no Accountant goes through the year without knowing how changes in Tax Law will affect their clients.

Neither should you. If you're not reading books, subscribing to newsletters, magazines, attending seminars and webinars, you're on autopilot and missing opportunities.

Abraham Lincoln once said that if he had eight hours to chop down a tree, he'd spend seven of them sharpening his axe. Time spent in preparation reduces effort and improves results!

The different types of Salespeople:

There are four different types. They are:

- The professional visitor
- The order taker
- The product pusher
- The trusted advisor

The professional visitor is the nice type. The one who drops in with news, information, brings the occasional gift, takes you to events but never asks for an order.

There may be a few industries where the professional visitor is a valuable employee, but I haven't found one yet.

The order taker is just that. He or she calls or visits regularly and just fills out an order for what you say you want. Occasionally these persons show you something new or leave a catalogue but are never pro-active. From an employer's perspective, they make quota, are stable and reliable but never set the world on fire.

Ideal for the task of filling display racks or restocking environments but should never be called upon to generate new clients.

The product pusher makes lots of sales, invariably creates loads of new customers but doesn't enjoy revisiting. The product pusher knows his script, delivers it, asks for an order, wins it or loses it.

This category is going to get you orders, but they're money motivated and driven almost solely by the numbers. They're unlikely to have a great deal of care for the customer or for the ongoing relationship.

They're useful to have around for a product where the customer gets visited only once. Typically, product pushers aren't good at follow-up and certainly not recommended where you're looking to a long-term relationship with repeat business.

The trusted advisor is the counsellor salesperson. This is the person who takes time to ask questions and listen to what the customer has to say.

They take time to develop the relationship, show a genuine interest in the customer and take a pro-active role in the promotion of new ideas.

The trusted advisor holds their clients in high esteem. He or she assists them in the growth and development of the business. They're hard to find and expensive to keep, but worth their weight in gold.

The aspect of sales that I find most fascinating is that the four-step process that you'll find outlined in the next chapter can be learned and applied universally to any product or service.

Once learned and understood, it can make all four types of salespeople more productive.

Remember

Relationships = Money.

You can't close a sale. You can only open the relationship.

Buyers will close the sale themselves.

Chapter 5

The TIPS Process and How to Make It Work for You

Since the advent of the internet, we're more educated about the products we buy than we were twenty years ago.

The internet allows us to research products and vendors more easily than ever before. The preponderance of catalogues thrust into our mailboxes makes us aware of product models and their specifications before we go shopping.

Consumers buy differently as a result. We don't fall for the cute lines and the manipulative process. And if we do, there are consumer protection laws to help us back out of our decisions.

Yet we still find pushiness and manipulation in all kinds of industries. It makes me wonder if those individuals have ever experienced the boot on the other foot.

Remember that to another business, you're a customer. You're not easily fooled; you don't fall for clichéd pitches and corny lines and neither will it.

Understand too that most buying decisions are made by women so if she's looking at a washing machine or car, talk to her, not her brother, father, or husband. They are there as a trusted advisor but it's her with whom you need to build the relationship.

She expects you to treat her with respect and courtesy. She's entitled to expect that you will take the time to make sure that what you recommend is right for her.

Like you, she's afraid of making a bad decision, of having family and friends laugh at her choice and of being stuck with a product or service that doesn't suit her needs, wants or desires.

Your role is to eliminate those fears by making the transaction as smooth, painless and as risk-free as possible.

The process that you're about to discover is a smooth, straightforward non-confrontational one that puts you, the vendor, on the same page as the buyer. In effect, because you end up seeing the situation in the same way as your buyer, it partners you together.

There are four key steps involved in this process. Each one must be accomplished in the correct sequence, and each must be completed before the next is started.

The steps are not measurable, and your prospect won't tell you when it's time to move on. It's a sense you must develop for yourself, and the best way is to get started with your very next prospect.

These four steps are simply explained and the way to recall them is the acronym **TIPS.**

T stands for Trust.
It represents gaining the buyer's trust and confidence in you and your company.

Remember these two phrases:

"What you are speaks so loudly, I can't hear a word you're saying."

And...

"You never get a second chance to make a first impression."

Trust starts from your first contact. This includes everything up to and including the first few minutes with your buyer. It may be a phone call, letter, personal introduction, or referral. How you present yourself will have a major factor on the trust established.

Here's a list of some of the things that can influence the first impression:

Your advertising (letterhead, press ads, literature, website.)

Your advertising must indicate that you're more interested in your customer than in yourself. When you run ads with your logo and Company name at the top and brag about how long you've been in business, you're not showing an interest in the customer.

When you replace your logo and name with a headline that appeals to the customer's problems, when your copy explains how you relate to the problem and can provide an appropriate solution, when you provide testimonials and a viable offer, you're helping establish trust.

One of the biggest mistakes made in ads is either not having a call to action or having the wrong one. The objective of any advert is to influence the audience to act; make a phone call, visit a store or visit a website.

The other big mistake is to ask potential customers to call for the best price. When you do that, you're painting yourself into a corner from which it's very hard to escape.

Your phone voice and manner

Unless the promotion asks them to phone for recorded information, answer the call in a friendly, proactive manner. Clearly understand that any incoming call could be from someone who's looking to spend money with you. The next call you answer may be the biggest, best prospect you've ever had—your dream client.

Please ensure that the people who take the call are trained. This is vital. You must be in control of the call. You should be asking the questions.

The first thing to do is make sure you identify yourself by giving the caller your name. Then gently obtain theirs.

Next, you need to ask a question that identifies their interest in your product. Get a conversation established that has them reveal why they're interested. Then and only then, take the call to the next stage.

This stage involves organising your preferred next action. That may be to have them visit you, or you them. It may be to send them a report, audio, sample, whatever.

Monitor the results. Test and measure which combination of phrases works best and use the most successful.

The conversion rate of incoming enquiry calls is one of the most crucial aspects of your business. These calls have cost you money to generate and the result is crucial to your success, and to the establishment of long-term trust.

Your dress-sense

Are you dressed appropriately for your product and for the market?

For example, if you're selling sophisticated software, and you call with a voice that says, "car mechanic"; trust is endangered.

Likewise, if you're selling car parts and you arrive at your customer's workshop in a three-piece black suit, white shirt and yellow silk tie, you're likely to be regarded with suspicion and caution.

I have a rule of thumb that says you should always dress at least to the level of your buyer, and preferably one level higher.

Your dress, irrespective of gender, should be appropriate for the market in which you work. Remember again, you never get a second chance to make a first impression. **Your** first impression goes a long way toward gaining trust.

Your accessories

Little things like clean shoes, tidy hair, subtle make-up, and jewellery make the difference. Pay attention to them.

What you are carrying

Carrying too much, "stuff" makes you look threatening. I go into most calls with a notepad in a leather folder. Try not to carry any more than that unless you've got a real reason to do so.

However, carrying nothing suggests that you don't care, so at least carry a decent-sized notebook so you can make notes.

The first few words you say when you meet the buyer

Don't rush in. Start gently, engage in some small talk, look, wait and feel for that moment when it's time to start talking shop.

Your stationery and website

Your letters need to be professionally presented. If you can't use a word processor, find someone who can and pay them to do your letters for you, or take a course in word processing. Pay a graphic artist to create a logo instead of doing it yourself with some drag and drop graphics package. Print your cards on a decent stock; flimsy homemade cards emerging from your inkjet imply uncertainty and a lack of confidence in your own business.

A website should be quick to load, easy to navigate and make it very easy for your customer to either buy directly from the site or to contact you. It's astounding how long it takes on most business websites to find the phone number or a link to email.

While on this one, please don't promote, "sales@...." admin@... Or, "info@...." if you want to provide personal service. *Why?* People like to deal with people. Why not put, "sally@...." or email our Sales Manager, Stephen Ford, "stephen.ford@..."

Better still, have a Contact Form on your website rather than a clickable email link. A clickable link can be read by those nasty crawlers spammers use and your email address with be flogged off to everyone wanting to sell you Viagra and African money scandals! If you must put an email address on your website, have your developer place it on the page in graphic format. That way it's less likely to be picked up by spammers.

You should also look to catch incorrect spelling. Make sure that, "damien@" also finds you if your name is, "Damian." The same applies to, "Steven and Stephen, Lesley and Leslie, and Jeff and Geoff." Maximise the possibility of their email reaching you.

I'm talking about *perceptions*, and even though you may be very capable, first impressions count. Don't risk what could be an excellent business transaction by jeopardising the establishment of trust.

Although there's more about websites in Chapter 6, if you're just starting out and don't have a website, at least register a domain name for yourself so your emails look professional. "PeterJackson@JacksonPartners.com" looks far more professional and delivers more trust and credibility than, "JacksonPartners@yahoo.com."

There's no excuse for your business not to have an email address at your domain name when Dot Com domain names are cheap to register at around $10 per year or around $20 per year for Australian .com.au domains. Hosting is inexpensive too, starting at around $10 per month.

I stands for Identify.
It relates to the ability to identify a problem or an issue your customers have that you can solve, or an opportunity with which you can excite them.

Trust must first be established so you can start to identify the real issues or problems. Identifying the real issue comes from asking questions, and you're going to meet resistance to your questions if you haven't first gained their trust.

Let's get this straight right from the start:

No one is going to buy anything of any real value from you unless doing so solves a problem for *him or her*. I'm not talking about the $2 chocolate bar you're selling as a fund-raiser for the local school or sports club. This is real life, business-to-business or person-to-person buying where serious money is changing hands.

And you must realise that at this stage, the potential customers may not even know the problem exists! You may have to help them recognise it.

In his book *The 7 Habits of Highly Effective People,* Stephen Covey says: *"Seek first to understand, then to be understood."*

What we are saying here is that to meet the client's need, you have to understand why that person has the need in the first place and help them to see that for themselves.

This process is explained in the next chapter.

P stands for <u>P</u>ropose.
It relates to your ability to propose an appropriate solution to their problem.

Your solution must be of value, and must either make or save money, or create pleasure or ease pain.

In days gone by, salespeople would use trick lines to embarrass folk into buying. The encyclopaedia salesperson would say things like, "If your children's education is important to you, you'll buy this for them."

Clearly, this style of conversation is manipulative and not focused on providing a solution. This style of selling doesn't work anymore. Especially not with consumer laws allowing mandatory cooling-off periods for buyers to cancel orders placed under duress.

Furthermore, you're a professional, and this is not the behaviour of a professional salesperson.

S stands for <u>S</u>et a timeline or establish a <u>S</u>ense of urgency.
It relates to your ability to set a timeline for the adoption of your solution.

Your role is to encourage your clients to see that the problem is urgent enough for them to react positively to your proposed solution. If not, then to give you a positive indication of when it will be implemented.

This is one occasion when you need to be focused. If your buyer says something like, "We'll proceed in the next Financial Year", you should be ready to respond with, "Great. Let's schedule a series of sessions before then to get everything ready. How does May 24 sound for the first?"

If the buyer accepts, you're done. The sale is made and you're both agreeing to an implementation strategy.

I sincerely believe that if you've successfully completed the previous three steps correctly, the only, "close" you'll ever need is the establishment of a timeline. That's why this book doesn't have a chapter on, "closing the sale"

If you're met with resistance when you are setting the timeline, sound a mental alarm. You've missed something along the way. It may be a put-off. Mentally backtrack to find out where you missed the clue or made a false assumption.

Every sale you complete shows that you have successfully navigated each of these four steps. Conversely, every time a sale is lost, it means you've missed a step.

Please understand; it's OK to miss a sale here and there, especially if you can learn from the experience. *(Your sales manager may disagree with me here!)*

Recognise that some sales aren't there to be made in the first place. The client may not have had a problem you could solve. Your very best solution may not have solved it. These are not lost sales. That's because you never had the sale to lose!

And here's a lesson in itself: Not every sale can be made.

Don't feel bad when one gets away from you. Simply look at what you did along the way. From the first contact onwards and ask yourself honestly if you succeeded in each of the four **T – I – P – S** steps.

If you're honest with yourself, you'll find the missing link.

Look back at the last sale that got away. What did you miss?

Look at every call, every new client meeting you will make from today on and ask yourself: Did I adequately cover each of these four steps along the way to completing this transaction?"

I vividly recall my first coaching session in 2001 with Stephen Bradshaw, founder of *sim*PRO, with whom I worked for several years from the very foundation of his now multinational company. Steve took to TIPS like a duck to water and within weeks his fledgling company had made its first sale.

Not only did he retain me to teach TIPS to his growing sales team, whenever his own sales dropped off, he would call me in for a refresher session and I would analyse where he was going wrong. As TIPS is a systemised process, it was easy for me to get him back on track, and yes, it always worked.

Shortly after the initial session I had with Steve, he asked me to write some adverts for them that would appear in the electrical trade magazines.

His earlier ads featuring a red toolbox and a few bullet points hadn't worked, yet when I presented him with a full-page, long copy advert with the headline, "Is your trade service business operating to its true potential?" he was sceptical.

The proof was in the eating as the phone started to ring from the day the first magazine hit the streets.

We took the copy from the article, built a new website and ran adverts to it using AdWords. (Google AdWords is now known as Google Ads, both are trademarks of Google, Inc.) The results were phenomenal. Sales enquiries just kept coming in. More staff were appointed, and they outgrew three offices in just six years.

Today *sim*PRO employs over 300 staff and has offices in five countries. They still use Google Ads to attract new business.

I teach all my sales coaching clients this process. It's fascinating that whenever one of them calls me for a pep talk because things aren't going as well as they should be, we find that they're shortcutting or eliminating one of the steps. Once they understand this and get back on track doing the four steps in the correct sequence, their sales take off again.

Remember

Take the sale one step at a time.

Use the TIPS acronym and track your results.

You can't measure what you don't record.

Chapter 6

How to Find Out Quickly What They Want to Buy

The second step is to help your customer identify her problem to the point where when you propose the appropriate solution, she wants to buy your product. Remember TIPS and review every sales call and every marketing campaign you create with these four steps in mind.

- Your ability to gain the buyer's **Trust** and confidence in you.
- Your ability to **Identify** a problem that you can solve.
- Your ability to **Propose** an appropriate solution.
- Your ability to **Set** a timeline.

(Notice how each of them contains the term "your ability"?)

When you get on the phone to your prospective customer, consider that she may be having a really bad day. If the initial reaction to your call is negative, the client may not be receptive to your message. It may be that something else has taken her focus at the time, and you have become an unwelcome intrusion.

Ask if she has a couple of minutes to talk right now, and if not, when would be a good time to call again. Learn to listen to the response you get. If it's terse, or if you're cut short, take the hint, and try again.

This isn't meant to be a course about telephone selling; there are plenty of them out there. However, what you will learn from this book are the techniques to use rather than the things to say. They will stand you in good stead when correctly implemented.

Communication is the *response* you get. It's what comes back when you say something. This basically means if you ask a silly question, you get a silly answer. In other words, you must learn to ask the right questions at the right time.

Here's the key point on communications...

Learn how to ask appropriate questions. I can't stress this one enough.

Here it is again... Learn how to ask appropriate questions.

There are three types of questions you can ask.

("Three?" I hear you ask. "I've only ever been taught about two.")

1. The closed question

These are questions that result in, 'yes or no, either/or' answers. Questions like

- "Did you want that in yellow or blue?"
- "Will that be cash or credit?"
- "Do you come here often?"

These questions are used to gain specific information and should be used sparingly. They are often used to confirm details such as, "Was that for the passenger or driver's side of the vehicle?" when told that the buyer wants an external mirror for their car.

Too many closed questions strung together in a sentence make recipients feel as though they are being cross-examined. It's uncomfortable for them, and certainly not very professional on your part.

2. The open question

Open questions ask for information. They are used to stimulate and encourage discussion.
Questions such as:

- "What are the key factors of your capital equipment replacement policy?"
- "Ideally, where would you like to relocate?"
- "When would it be appropriate to schedule our next session?"
- "How does your company react to negative publicity?"

Open questions require clients to reveal details about themselves or about the topic of discussion.

Open questions begin with the words "Who, what, when, where, why and how".

These questions should be used far more frequently than closed questions (unless you're a detective!) They take practice, however, and a sign of an unskilled or lazy salesperson is their all too frequent use of the closed question.

Practice the art of open questions, and you'll be very pleasantly surprised at the outcome.

3. The "Tell me about" question

This is the question you ask when you're not asking a question.

When you start with, "Tell me about...", you remove the question's emphasis. It makes the question conversational, less threatening and the recipient feels more at ease.

Because it's conversational, the result is that you get more information than you would with an open question.

There are ways to vary this. You can prefix the phrase with, "So" to make it, "So, tell me about..." or you can substitute the word, "about" with, 'who, what, when, where, why, or how.' Another variant is, "Talk to me about..."

If you watch experienced TV journalists, you'll see this technique used widely.

Here's an example of how it works. "Tell me about your staff superannuation scheme", is likely to result in you gaining a massive amount of information. As you listen, you might want to get some specifics about certain aspects of the answer.

If so, ask something like, "And can your staff choose to have a higher rate of superannuation deducted from their salary if they want?" and you will get a, 'yes' or 'no' response, perhaps with a little more added detail.

Sentences that begin with, "Tell me about" don't have a question mark at the end. The result is that it appears not to be a question. It's non-threatening. And that's exactly what we're looking to achieve, a non-threatening conversation.

If you adopt nothing else from this book, adopt the, "Tell me about" questioning process. It works in every sales environment you can imagine. Professional services, hard products, wholesale, retail and everywhere.

To find out how devastatingly effective this is, say to a co-worker or your significant other, "Tell me about your day" then shut up while they tell you far more than intended.

Let me share two examples with you...

When I was that stripling youth on the farm, we required a gearbox for a vehicle. I called the parts shop and said I needed a gearbox for my Ford. The salesperson went on to ask me a series of closed questions about my car. Was it an `84 model? Was it this; was it that?

I finally got the answer I wanted (price and availability) and rang another business to get a check price. (My boss told me to get more than one quote...) Their salesperson said, "*Tell me about your Ford, mate*".

I told him the year, model, etc. He replied straight away with a closed question, "Manual or automatic gearbox?"

It was a manual, I told him. He responded with the price and availability, and then asked me if I wanted it delivered, or did we want them to fit it?

Three appropriate questions and he made the sale. It's a lesson I've never forgotten.

The second case was while presenting a sales course for a recruitment company. One of the attendees, Sean, had recently joined the firm and during the first break, just before I taught them the questioning process I said to the owner, "How much do you know about Sean?"

"Quite a bit I reckon" he answered.

"I'll bet you $100 that I can find out more about him in the next 15 minutes than you know."

The bet was on and shortly after the break I said to Sean, "You're new here aren't you Sean; why not tell us about yourself?"

With little prompting we heard where he was born, why his family moved to Australia from New Zealand, where he went to school, his junior sporting successes, the car accident that seriously injured his brother and that his mother drank too much!

The $100 quietly changed hands over lunch.

How I got this client is an interesting story. The introduction was by referral which I received by phone at about 4 on a January Monday afternoon. I planned to call the prospect the next morning yet at 4:30, he called me and asked why I hadn't called?

I figured his issue was urgent, so we agreed to meet the following afternoon at 3:30pm. I told him I had to be across town to run a training session by 5:30 so needed to leave by 4:30. On arrival, I was ushered into a meeting room and quickly realised this guy was competitive and had an ego.

Every wall had pictures of him winning or being awarded something. They went back to his schoolboy Rugby days!

He walked in 5 minutes later and after the handshakes I asked him this question: Tell me which of these you're most proud of" pointing around the room. That answer took 20 minutes. I sat and listened. Then I asked, "So tell me why I'm here."

For another 20 minutes, I sat and listened. Basically, the response was that he wasn't happy with the performance of his sales team and felt they could use some training. At the end of his exhaustive reply, he asked me what I could do.

I quickly gave him an outline of a program and said it would be about $7,000, and when did he want me to do it?

He then went on about how he was selling his house, his wife was pregnant with their third child, he was getting the office painted; would I put my proposal in writing, and could I do it in June?

I was by now very concerned about meeting my 5:30 commitment so I agreed and made my farewells. I was just walking out of the office when I turned around and asked, "Have you thought about how many sales and how much profit waiting until June will cost you?"

There was no response, so I drove off. The next morning there was an email from him. It read: "Money is good, send invoice, book us in to start second week in Feb."

I immediately wrote a thank you email, gave him a start date, and sent the invoice with 10 days to pay. Five minutes later there was a reply simply saying, "Paid."

It was an immensely successful program. His sales improved within days of its completion and he sent me a very nice, very expensive bottle of Scotch as a, "well done" gift. What's significant is that in a meeting that lasted an hour, I spoke for maybe five minutes and asked only three questions – and the last almost as an afterthought.

I was running my sales training program, "How to Gain and Retain More Customers" on a regular basis. Over ten years, I had trained a significant number of people and about a year after doing the program for the HR firm, the owner called me to ask if I knew a guy called John?

John had done my course and had listed it on his resume in applying for a job with him! He got the job and was very successful. John went on to later start his own labour-hire company, selling it years later for a very tidy sum. He credits the twin barrels of TIPS and Consequence for his success.

Your first exercise is to start using open and, "Tell me about" questions more often. The risk you take here is that if you don't listen and take in the answer, you won't benefit.

Remember: You have two ears and one mouth so use them in that order

You see, if you're used to asking closed questions, you will be used to hearing short, precise answers. Now that you're asking open questions, you will have to listen more intently to collect the gems of information you need to identify problems you can solve.

Then you must learn how to advocate urgent action to solve them. *(I mentioned that you'd have some work to do.)*

Write down questions that you could ask your buyers that would assist you to gain a better understanding of their needs and problems. Here are some clues that might help; typical questions that work in almost any situation.

- What are the best things about how you do this now?
- How would you change things if you could?
- If you could mimic another system, which (or who's) would you mimic?
- Who would you suggest would be the most suitable person to lead this project?
- Tell me how you would achieve this outcome if money were no object.

Before you run off to practice asking these questions, here's one more piece of advice. And one more set of important questions.

These questions will help you avoid much embarrassment and heartbreak.

They will help you make sure you aren't trying to sell to someone who can't make the buying decision. And after all, you can't get a buying decision from someone who hasn't the authority to make the purchase, can you?

Here are a couple of samples for you:

- Tell me about your company's decision-making process for purchases of this kind.
- Tell me who else will be involved in deciding to adopt this solution.

I'm sure you can think of many similar questions to ask that will help you reveal information about your client's wants and needs.

I'm frequently asked how you string open, closed and tell-me-about questions together in a conversation.

Until recently, I'd not analysed that in any detail and so I wouldn't have been able to answer the question.

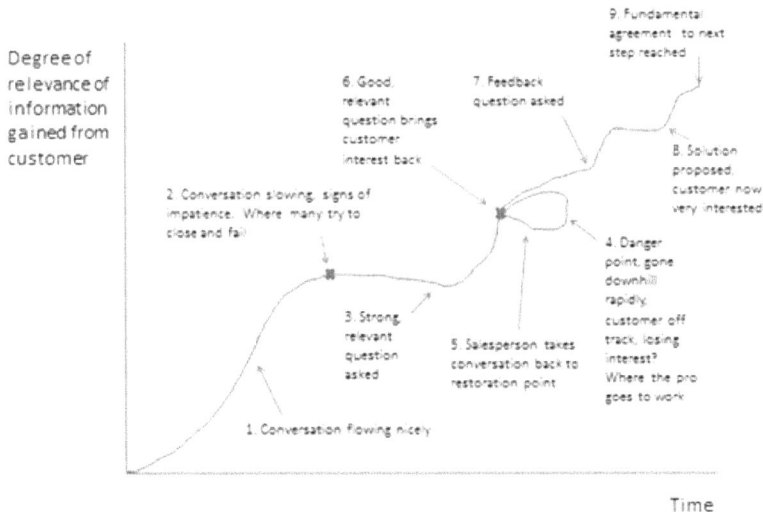

Frankly, I'd not consciously focused on a specific process or sequence. It had been somewhat instinctive; the focus was simply on using them in a combination that delivered me the answers I sought.

However, over the last few years, I have analysed the combinations and if there is a rhythm, it's to start with a, "Tell–me-about" followed by a closed or confirming question, which is followed by an open question.

There certainly aren't hard and fast rules. Use them yourself until you see what works best for you.

I'd encourage you to go back over this section about asking questions, especially the, "Tell-me-about" because it's one of the three most important parts of the verbal sales process.

Let me show you pictorially how this works...

I call this, "The Conversation Graph" and it shows how a sales conversation should go. Most salespeople have no concept of how this works. They jump into the conversation with ears closed, seeking to "pitch" their idea or product without consideration of the client's position or situation.

At point 2 after they have pitched and failed, they run into objections and try to answer them. No matter what anyone tries to tell you about objections; if you're getting them, you're likely to have already missed the sale.

Remember

Your ability to make the sale depends upon your ability to identify a solvable problem.

Help your prospective customer to identify the problem by asking the right questions.

Chapter 7

How to Make Your Proposal Sound like Music to Their Ears

The easiest way to make a sale is to sell what they want to buy.

By using the first two steps of the TIPS process, you have now established enough trust to ask the questions to identify their problems, dreams, issues, or aspirations.

Once you're absolutely sure you understand the need, and they have downloaded all the information they need to tell you so they feel you have listened to them and really understand their challenge, you can present your product or service as the most appropriate solution.

You must do this in a fashion that highlights the most significant, most relevant aspects of how what you do makes a difference to your client.

What are you really offering your client, and how do you know that it's relevant? Here are some examples to help you:

You're selling patios
She wants an outdoor entertaining area where the kids can play and make a mess or where she can entertain her friends in the cool of a summer evening or when it's raining.

You build retaining walls
He needs something to stop the landfill above his house from sliding into his pool when it rains heavily.

You're an accountant providing Tax Reporting
Clients wants to make sure they comply with tax legislation, so they don't get audited, hit with the stress of nuisance phone calls and letters and incur unexpected heavy fines.

You're a software salesperson selling databases
Your clients need a database to help them stay in touch with their clients, to record what they bought and when, so they can upsell them later.

You're a travel agent offering packaged holidays
They want a family holiday so they can relax, recharge and renew the family relationships. They want to be far away from email and the phone. They want a memory to last a lifetime.

You're a business coach
The clients want someone they can trust to help them successfully navigate the minefield of business decisions with the comfort of knowing you've been there yourself in a business of your own.

Beware of the process aspects of what you do. They're boring. They're unemotional and uninspiring. They're also not what your client wants. They require the emotional benefits and solutions your service brings.

There is an exercise on Page 5 of the workbook (jamesyuille.com/WYLTSWorkbook) for you to define this for your business.

You must refer to the issues they've raised in answer to your questions when illustrating how your solution works for them.

Getting clients comes down to identifying what you have to offer them that solves their problem or provides pleasure and then packaging your advertising, marketing and presentations to meet that need.

You are essentially a problem solver, and the problem is the gap between where your client is and where they want to be, or what they have and what they want to have.

You're in business to provide a solution to stop their pain or assist their pleasure. Your role is to identify the pain or the desired pleasure and meet or exceed their expectations with your offer.

By asking astute questions and listening attentively to their answers, you can identify the issues with which they are concerned. But what are, "astute questions"?

These are questions that help you establish what's going on in their business or in their personal lives.

The simple motivators behind all decisions are gaining pleasure and/or avoiding pain. In business, we'll most often hear this expressed as making or saving money. People are more motivated to avoid pain than gain pleasure so for best results, drive home the inevitable pain occasioned from not implementing your solution.

Ask yourself this question right now: "How does what I sell help to generate pleasure or assist in avoiding pain?"

Then ask this: "How does what I do add value?"

(This might be a knockout punch to you but let me tell you this straight: if what you do doesn't add value, people won't come to you.)

With those answers, you're ready to take on the world.

Sell benefits and added value.

When you build a patio, you take timber and make an outdoor entertaining area the whole family will enjoy for years.

When you help my family book holidays, you help us to bond and to create memories. (I can still remember my childhood family holidays like the one where I learned to swim in the clear, calm, unpolluted warm water of Lake Como in Italy. So much more inviting than the cold North Sea near my birthplace in Yorkshire!)

When you photograph my wedding, you are recording an historical event – the creation of a new family.

Each one of the strengths you've documented about your product is (I hope) factual. They may be impressive to you, but on their own, stated or in writing, they are unlikely to make you a sale. These facts are what we call, **features**.

They describe specific physical attributes of the product and its performance. They are if you like, the specifications. To someone other than an engineer or technician (we'll come to them shortly), these statements tend to be boring.

Here's how you test the hypothesis. If you tell me something about what you sell, and I can respond with, *"So what"*, you've delivered me a cold, hard, unemotional fact, a feature. By itself, it's meaningless.

When you read the point above about the outdoor entertaining area it probably didn't conjure up any real feeling. When you read the story I used to illustrate from my own childhood family holidays, it's likely to evoke an emotional chord with you. Your prospects are the same; they also respond more to emotion than logic. In fact, people generally make decisions emotionally and back them up with logic to justify their purchases.

Think about the favourite handbag, or your air-ride joggers; chances are they weren't the cheapest you could have bought but your purchase was influenced by looks, style, colour comfort and the confidence they afforded you; likewise with your watch, car, TV...

Dress it up in a fashion that gets them interested.

I took my elderly mother to buy a new cordless telephone as the buttons were too small for her to read and difficult to use with arthritic fingers. In the store, we were told about functions such as speed-dialling, three-way conversation capability, silent-alert, voice- recording, distance of signal, calling number display and battery life.

She looked vacant and disinterested, then simply said to the salesperson, "Show me one with big, raised buttons that I can easily see and that I can feel myself pressing."

The point was that nothing else mattered to her, just the big buttons she could easily see, and feel herself clicking as she dialled. You see, like most of us, Mum wasn't too interested in technical specifications.

Let me say that again. What the customer wants to hear from you is what your product or service will do for him and her in response to their stated needs.

My late father was an old-fashioned General Practitioner. I once asked him what made a good doctor. He replied by saying they had to remember that prescription without diagnosis is malpractice.

He went on to explain it like this…

"Imagine" he said, "that you came to my surgery and before you said anything, I told you that you had severe appendicitis and needed immediate surgery. I'm going to get my nurse to call an ambulance, book an operating theatre, an anaesthetist, and a surgeon; we're getting it out today!

"You look at me in horror and ask how I reached that conclusion?

"The way you're grimacing and holding your stomach.

"No, that's the onion on the burger I had for lunch repeating on me. I'm here about a badly ingrown toenail."

One very embarrassed doctor who pitched a solution on an assumption!

Unless you've made the mistake of boring them witless with an endless procession of facts about what you're selling, they aren't going to ask you to tell them what the product will do for them *(what problem it will solve)*. Unless they ask the question out of sheer frustration, that is.

They won't say directly, "Tell me how this widget will solve my critical manpower shortage." You must tell them. And they will only be interested if what it does helps them solve a problem (which you of course have brought to their attention).

Think about every decision you've made, in terms of either the avoidance of pain or the gaining of pleasure. Doubtless, every single decision was made for one or other of these reasons. In the majority of circumstances, more people will make a decision that avoids pain above making a decision that gains pleasure.

Remember too, that most decisions are made based upon emotions and then backed with rationality. What it means to you, the salesperson is that even though you're going to give the buyer lots of emotional reasons for dealing with you, you still need to support your argument with logic and rationale.

Production managers will decide to purchase something that will save them time (and therefore money) in the production process, so long as the investment made does not exceed the savings to be gained.

Their emotional reasoning (pleasure vs. pain) is that the decision will make them look good in the eyes of their superiors (gain pleasure by means of recognition). Or, they may have avoided pain, as they would have needed to lay off two people had they not found a way to save money elsewhere (by using your solution).

A sales manager will invest in advertising if the campaign costs less than the expected profit to be gained from the resulting increase in sales.

Work out the scenarios for each of your own potential customers. Ask yourself this question every time you speak to buyers:

"Am I showing customers how to gain pleasure or avoid pain, or make or save them time or money with this transaction?"

Equate everything you do commercially with these criteria, too; "Is what I'm about to do going to make or save someone time or money?" (A closed question, by the way.) If the answer is, 'no,' think seriously about why you're going to do it.

Price is not always the driving issue. Price is the issue only when there is no other consideration on which to base the decision. As an Insurance Broker, your client may have a fleet of cars, and be asking about renewals.

You explain a policy that provides that person with a loan vehicle within 12 hours of receiving the claim, and how the loan vehicle is theirs until the damaged one is repaired.

This means that their staff member isn't off the road, and that they won't have an argument with the Insurer about paying for the loan car.

Explained properly, this policy's additional premium will be considered trivial and the client should make the decision to buy.

You have explained the benefits of spending a little more, and along the way, differentiated yourself from the other broker vying for the business.

I vividly remember an advertising campaign run for Johnnie Walker Scotch Whiskey, which asked, "Which would you rather: the Scotch you'd rather pay for or the Scotch you'd rather drink?" Those words haunt me every time I go to a liquor outlet.

Let me introduce you to a unique twist on a common theme.

I'm sure you've heard of, 'Features and Benefits.'

I found that these two steps weren't adequate when explaining what a product did for the client. It needed extending to get an "aha" response, so I created a 4 step process which I call 'The Theory of Consequence'.

The Theory of Consequence is the single most important element of this book and most salespeople don't even know it exists. I discovered this idea sitting in my bedroom as a 21-year-old figuring out why my prospects would want to buy my product. I've rarely found anyone alluding to it in the plethora of marketing materials that come across my desk, and it gained me an unexpected speaking spot at the Jay Abraham conference in LA.

Even those few who know it exists don't generally understand its significance in sales conversations.

The acronym for The Theory of Consequence is F-F-B-C. These initials stand for, Feature, Function, Benefit and Consequence.

Take time to read and re-read this chapter. Your mastery of the Theory of Consequence will likely result in thousands of dollars of sales and profits, dollars and profits made more quickly and easily than you've ever made them before.

Let's examine each of the F-F-B-C terms individually.

A Feature is a fact about something. A design element if you prefer. The handle on your coffee mug is a feature. The pocket clip on your pen and the light in the fridge are both features of those items.

How do we turn features into words a buyer wants to hear?

We need to express them as benefits, using words that explain what the feature will do for the client. How it will make or save time or money.

But wait, there's another very necessary process to go through first. We need to understand the term, 'Function.' The function is what the feature does or allows you to do.

One function of the handle on your coffee mug is to provide ease of holding the hot mug.

A function of the clip on your pen is to allow you to clip the pen onto your clothes.

The function of the light in your fridge is to illuminate the inside of your fridge.

Next, we look at, 'Benefits.' Now we're starting to talk their language! Benefits are what the features and the functions mean to the buyer.

The benefits of the handle on the mug include preventing us from burning fingers when we pick it up and providing us with a firm grip to avoid spilling the drink on ourselves.

The clip on your pen means it won't easily fall out of your pocket and get lost or damaged, meaning you won't need to be replacing it regularly.

The light in the fridge allows you to tell the juice bottle from the vinegar bottle in the middle of the night (or the beer from the chocolate sauce!)

Each of your product's features will have several benefits, and the benefit will vary depending upon your audience.

Finally, let's examine the Consequence of the feature, function and benefit. Very few professional salespeople, even amongst the most seasoned, ever come to grips with this concept.

Sometimes expressed as, "What this really means to you is", the consequence is the main purpose for buying the item. In other words, the consequence is the emotional gain benefiting you from owning the item.

The consequence of the handle on the mug is that it will save you from scalds, *(saves you from pain)* or from having to repeat your work if you spill the contents *(saves you time)*.

The consequences of the clip on your pen are that you won't easily lose it *(saving you money)* and whenever you need to write something down, you always know where your pen is. No need to hunt around or bother other people; its right where it always is. Now, whenever you have the need to write down that all-important phone number, you can.

You're out with a client and you have an agreement in principal and the next step is a signature on the contract, you don't have a pen, the customer doesn't have one; how much easier is it for them to say they'll take it away to sign and return later.? Instead, you reach into your handbag or pocket and there's your pen. Deal done!

I'll let you work out the consequence of knowing the difference between the vinegar and the juice bottles in the fridge when you're half-asleep!

Insurance people have been using this sequence on, "Feature – Function – Benefit – Consequence" for years when selling life insurance.

It goes like this:

"Buying this cover will give you $1,000,000 death cover on your partner, **(feature)** and we will pay it out to you and your children on your partner's death **(function)**.

It will allow you to pay out your outstanding debts **(benefit)** and will let you start the rest of your life without money worries **(consequence)**. You can still send your children to the schools you want, to pay the mortgage and have regular family holidays."

In effect, the consequence is the result they get when your solution is applied to their problem. What they're buying is the consequence, what you're selling is the feature.

Let me make another point here. Decisions are made emotionally and backed with logic. Not the other way around.

Technical people especially, make the mistake of selling with logic instead of with emotion. Thousands of sales are missed for the simple reason that the emotions of the buyer are ignored.

It's simple. If we made every decision logically, we'd all be driving $2,000 bomb cars, wearing no-name brand clothes, holidaying in tents and carrying our goods and chattels in plastic bags.

Why? Because logically, these are the cheapest solutions to cars, clothes and travel.

If this were the case, the Porsche, Nike, Marriott and Louis Vuitton brands wouldn't exist. We can't logically defend our purchase of any of these brands but justifying them emotionally is easy.

Let me share with you some of the ways I've used Consequence to make easy sales.

Remember the telephone answering machines story?

Functionally an answering machine is a tape recorder fastened to a telephone line. It announces your absence and allows callers to record a message for you.

The benefit is that it answers your phone when you can't.

The consequences are multiple.

You can still take incoming business calls even when you're working on site, when your wife is at the bank, shopping, or collecting the kids from school.

Your advertising becomes more effective because your callers can still leave messages for you.

You don't miss jobs simply because you weren't there to take the call. You're now more flexible and potentially more effective and more profitable and you can call people back who you otherwise wouldn't know had tried to call you.

Now let's use a consequence to create our headline. Here is the one that we found most successful:

How to Answer Every Customer Call – Even When You're Out.

Notice that I said this was the one we found to be most successful. We knew that because we tried several different headlines. Some worked better than others; this was the best.

Let's see how we apply this by looking further into the coffee cup example. Assume you're the buying authority for a major hotel. You have hundreds, maybe thousands of coffee cups; none have handles because nobody has ever thought of putting a handle on a coffee cup before.

If I called you (as the salesperson for this new cup) and asked for a meeting to show you cups with handles, your response would likely be, 'No.'

Now, imagine the same scenario where I call to say I have an idea to share with you about a way to reduce or eliminate the spillage of coffee, the cost and effort of cleaning stains off tablecloths, chairs, carpets, bedspreads, staff uniforms etc. and at the same time, reduce the likelihood of legal action by customers who have spilled hot drinks on themselves and endured pain or discomfort.

You might want to talk with me, yes?

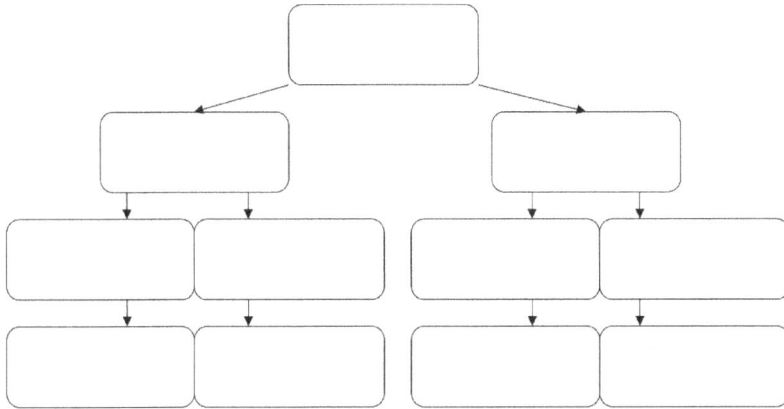

You see, what I'm doing is selling the consequence. And get this: The consequence is the exact reverse of their problem.

See where T-I-P-S fits in? Identify their problem. Propose an appropriate solution.

The consequence becomes your headline.

The feature is the logic; the consequence is the emotion. Remember, they buy based on emotions and support the decision with logic. They buy the function.

This is one step beyond benefits. Benefits aren't the whole deal. It's like driving without using top gear.

Remember that one feature may have three functions; a function may have five benefits and a benefit three consequences.

When you start to work the F-F-B-C process out for your product, use a mind-map; it's easier.

Understand this and you'll leapfrog any competitor. Guaranteed.

This graphic is a mind map allowing you to develop a series of functions, benefits and consequences for your service.

Write a feature of your product in the top box, and then in each of the two on the second row, write different functions.

Row three is for benefits and row four for consequences.

Please do this exercise; it will make a huge impact on your results. You can find it on Page 6 of the workbook (jamesyuille.com/WYLTSWorkbook).

Another successful example of consequence was when I sold coil binding and laminating machines for GBC. This was some years ago when laminating machines weren't common office products.

I identified that when you laminated and coil-bound business quotes, they looked and felt great, a cut above how they would otherwise look. I figured that progressive companies in competitive industries would like to have their quotes and presentations stand out from the crowd.

Sales managers were the obvious entry point and so I phoned and asked them this question:

"If I could show you a way to get your quote to the top of the pile, to look superior to your competitor's, would it be worth ten minutes of your time to see how it's done?"

I used this line repeatedly. The conversion rate of call-to-meeting was huge, and sales were too.

All I did was show them a sample, which was made up of a coil-bound and laminated letter addressed to them with details of the machines and their costs.

All I'd say was, "How would you like your proposals to look like this?"

These were some of the quickest and easiest sales I ever made. The back end was nice too as I received ongoing commissions for the coil and laminating film used in the machines.

GBC also had a mini-laminating machine. It was designed to laminate photo ID cards and we didn't sell many of them.

One day, that all changed. It was at the time VHS and BETA video recorders were becoming affordable and video libraries were just starting to appear.

I had a VHS recorder and went into a video library to find out how it worked. The owner explained the process and showed me the membership card he issued. It was just a business-sized card, printed with his logo and he wrote the customer details on the back.

I remarked that he'd have high turnover of cards because they'd get damaged and worn in people's pockets and purses, or when they went through washing machines.

"Yes" he agreed, "but what else can I do?" I had a laminated business card in my pocket and showed it to him. I explained how it was impervious to moisture and lasted almost forever. It was exactly what he needed.

"How can I get that?" he asked.

Inside five minutes I had an order for a machine and 1,000 laminating pouches. He bought thousands more pouches and referred me to dozens of other owners of video stores. They all bought.

Today's equivalent is the sale of a plastic loyalty or membership cards instead of cardboard ones. An international coffee shop chain sells you a plastic card. When you buy it, you get a voucher for a free coffee and one of their other premium drink products. In addition to that, when you register the card online, there's a credit that covers your next purchase. They swipe your card at every purchase and tell you on the spot your accumulated redeemable cash balance.

Consequence applied to problem results in a solution.

Consequence allows you to step apart from the sellers of commodities.

Consequence empowers you to differentiate on price.

Consequence enabled me to sell millions of dollars in facsimile machines for NEC in the 80's. I used a $5 disposable component of the machine for this one.

Fax machines started to replace Telex machines in the mid-80's. One of the biggest objections buyers raised was fraud. They were concerned that staff would fax sensitive files to unauthorised recipients, and they would have no way of knowing.

Our top-line machine sold for over $6,000. It had a little red rubber stamp feature that placed a tiny circular red mark at the top and bottom of every page that went through the machine.

I simply asked if security was an issue with them, and if it was, I said the NEC machine was the only one with a built-in fraud detector. I explained how the presence of the red circle on a document showed them that it had been sent somewhere by fax.

It sold hundreds of machines, making me tens of thousands of dollars in commissions.

You should know that this machine was bigger, heavier, uglier, and more expensive than any other machine on the market. Yet armed with the Theory of Consequence, I was able to identify an issue of concern and paint my solution as highly desirable.

It was no longer a commodity. An emotional issue was addressed and the decision to spend more on this machine than others was logically defended.

I had a huge success with a direct-mail campaign to sell these machines. We were successful in winning a major contract to supply the State Government with fax machines.

Just a few days after the contract was let, I sent a letter to every school in Queensland with an overprint on the envelope. It read, "Handing this envelope to your school's principal could save your school $1,100"

The letter explained that we had just won the supply contract and although they wouldn't have seen it published yet, they could get our $3,000 machine for just $1,900 on this contract.

It generated a 38% response inside 30 days.

All we did was highlight the biggest, most significant consequence we could muster and published it as the headline.

What consequences can you offer?

When you closely examine your product and look at the consequences of every aspect of it, you too will move away from the commodity style offerings of your competitors.

Understand that the process first requires you to identify the issues then use the relevant consequences of your offer to bring home your differential.

You will see from this illustration that the consequence varies depending upon the situation.

You are selling a very expensive machine into a manufacturing environment. As part of the sale, you have to gain support from a variety of players within the customer's business. Each has a different concern.

- The operator wants to make sure his job is safe; that this new machine still needs people to operate it.
- The maintenance department wants to know if they need extra training and tools to maintain it.
- The IT department wants to know if it needs any new software or if it will integrate into their current CAD and reporting programs.
- Marketing wants to know what competitive advantage the product it makes give them.
- Finance wants to know how to pay for it.
- The MD wants to know about the return on investment.

You need to answer all these questions.

Knowing the consequence of ownership of your product is crucial.

This is beyond benefits; it's about results.

I've workshopped this as an interactive game in many training sessions with significant mindset change as the consequence. It's a key consulting discussion point as well.

I was consulting with a bed-and-breakfast establishment that was promoting a green, environmental message. They were telling me that visitors loved the quiet, pristine environment, the tropical birds, and the calm, tranquil waters lapping at the shore.

I interjected, "But they don't come for that, they come to escape the dramas of everyday life, to reconnect, to have breakfast in bed, to escape the kids and to make love. Everything else is a bonus." My intervention earned praise.

I am firmly of the opinion that "green" doesn't sell. I use this exercise in my workshops to illustrate why.

You have two rubbish bins at your house. One is for general rubbish, the other for recycling. The truck comes every Monday morning and empties both. On Sunday afternoon you have a huge party and there are too many empty cans and bottles to fit in the recycling bin. Do you:

- Keep them aside for next week's collection?
- Ask a neighbour if you can put them in her recycling bin?
- Put the junk into the general rubbish bin?

I've posed this scenario hundreds of times and most people say they would put them into the general rubbish bin. I ask why and the common response is that they don't see that it matters too much.

How you can explain your expensive solution in what appears to be a price-conscious marketplace?

Imagine you're a householder wanting to contract a painter to paint your home. You call three painters and invite them to price the job.

The first arrives in a paint-splotched, tired vehicle, wanders vaguely around your home making notes on the back of his hand and says, "Well lady, it'll be $3,500. Phone if you want me to do the job," he says as an afterthought, leaving a ragged homemade business card on your table.

The second arrives in a clean, tidy, sign-written vehicle, takes notes on a clipboard, asks a few questions about your colour scheme and leaves you a neat, crisp, hand-written quote form with a price of $4,700.

The first two are dressed as you'd expect; overalls covered in paint. At least the second one took his shoes off before he entered your house!

The third arrives in a clean, shiny car. He's dressed in business clothes with a logo on his shirt. He removes his shoes, enters and starts to talk with you about your family, your lifestyle and how you use the spaces. He looks carefully at each room, takes measurements and discusses the colour scheme.

Taking his time, he uses a calculator to work out the figures and then starts to explain his offer:

"Mrs. Thomas, here's what's going to happen when we paint your home: on Sunday, a guy from Dogsmart will arrive to take your dogs to the kennel for a week — we do that because dogs simply hate the smell and they react badly to household disruption; they'll be well cared for, washed, and groomed before they're returned.

"On Monday morning, our prep team will be here to remove the paintings and objects d'art and make sure all of your furniture is protected by drop sheets. An hour or two later, our professionals will arrive to start the sanding process. That will take all day Monday and the dust will all be vacuumed away by the time you get home.

"Tuesday is when we start the undercoat. Let me tell you, this is the worst day. The smell is dreadful, and you won't want to be here that night. So, at about 6pm, a limo will arrive to take everyone to the best hotel in town where your stay and all meals are provided.

"Wednesday morning the kids will be taken direct to school in the limo and you to work.

"Wednesday to Friday we'll be painting everything. Ceilings, walls, doors; it will be a hive of activity let me tell you. Friday afternoon two trucks will arrive; one is our carpet cleaner who will clean the carpets and soft furnishings; the other will be the curtain cleaners to remove your curtains, clean them overnight and deliver them on Saturday morning.

"The dogs will return on Saturday too. By midday you'll be back to normal in your clean, freshly painted home.

"The following Friday, our quality inspector will arrive to make sure everything is to your satisfaction. He'll check for any imperfections, any missed spots and for any paint that's where it shouldn't be. Whatever he finds will be fixed for free.

"Every six months for the next five years, we'll return and fix any chips, scratches or accidents again for free. We want your home to look as good in five years as it did on the day we finished here.

"Mrs Jackson, all this is done for you for just $6,760 and at $65 per week, our payment plan means you pay no interest for two years.

"When do you want us to start?"

Did you want him to paint your home? The job was really no different and the costs similar. The kennelling for two dogs for a week wasn't much as he has a permanent booking. Tuesday is the limo driver's gentlest evening and he does a deal too. He has a club membership at the hotel and Tuesday is the quietest night. The carpet and curtain cleaning are again bulk deals. They're joint venture partners anyway as his brother-in-law owns both businesses...

All in all, the additional costs are maybe $1,000 - $1,200. The point is that he created a point of difference.

20% of people will always buy the cheapest solution.

20% will always buy the dearest solution.

Most businesses compete for the 60% in the middle because nobody wants to be the cheapest and most don't know how to sell being the most expensive.

Wouldn't you rather play at the most expensive end of the marketplace?

Remember

You must create a point of difference.

If there are two or more of you doing the same thing, at least one of you is redundant.

Take the painter example and see how you can create a point of difference your clients will crawl over shards of glass to have you provide.

There is an exercise on Page 7 of the workbook (jamesyuille.com/WYLTSWorkbook) to help you do this.

Chapter 8
Questions You Must Answer Before You Move Forward

By now you should be looking at your product and your business from the customer's perspective. You should be examining the consequences of ownership of your product or service.

Take time for a reality check here. Think about these questions for a minute.

- Do your customers see your business the way you do? Yes / No
- Do they see your strengths in the same way you do? Yes / No
- Is your offer appealing? Yes / No
- Does your offer provide them with a low or risk-free entry point? Yes / No
- Do they see your payment terms as advantageous or disastrous? Yes / No
- Do they see your service department as an effective and efficient ally, or as surly and unhelpful? Yes / No
- As the salesperson, are you adequately informed about your business and able to make decisions on the spot to help your clients? Yes / No
- If not, do you have to keep running back to your management team for answers and policy decisions? Yes / No

You can answer these questions on Page 8 of the workbook (jamesyuille.com/WYLTSWorkbook).

These issues all count towards the customer's level of trust and confidence in you and your business.

One of the often-quoted reasons for McDonald's success is their consistency.

Why do we go to McDonalds? Is it for the food? Is it for the service *(how many other restaurants do you go to where you're expected to clear the table yourself?)* or is it because of the consistency of experience and the marketing draw?

If you're in a strange place, or in a hurry, at least you know what to expect and it's always the same. Can your customers say the same about dealing with you?

How many alternative sources do they have for the same products or services? Why do your customers come to you? Is the experience consistent?

- Do you always answer the phone with the same message?
- Does the person answering the phone at lunchtime use the same script and answer with the same friendliness?
- What unique proposition do you offer?
- What service or product guarantee do they get from you?

A regular client of mine used to email me prior to the appointment to remind me of the meeting. He stopped after he realised that when I said I'd be somewhere or do something, he could rely on it happening or being done. There was no need to remind me.

Can your customers say the same about you?

These are the weaknesses with which you need to deal. You should prioritise them and immediately begin the fix as they will bring undone everything else you do. Similarly, threats should be confronted too.

Identify threats as perceived or real. Those that are real should be identified as immediate or future and dealt with accordingly. Perceived threats are just things that might happen. Be aware of them; examine the circumstances under which they might happen, and should those circumstances arise, examine them again and act.

It's also important to know the time cycle of your product.

Every product has a time cycle. The time cycle is the period between when this sale is made and the next time the buyer will buy the item. Knowing the time cycle means you don't attempt to sell someone when they aren't in the market.

If you have just bought a new car or a new dishwasher, you aren't going to be interested in buying another for a period of years. However, when the cycle is nearing completion, you will begin to look at advertising, read consumer magazines and start browsing suppliers for information.

Consider your computer. If it's a Mac, chances are that you've been encouraged back to their store or dealership for maintenance or software updates. At the very least, you've registered for iTunes and received news and information about new products. Everyone knows when Apple releases something new and most owners are keen to regularly upgrade. Three years is a long time to hold on to a Mac product.

On the other hand, if, like me, you're a PC user, it's highly unlikely the vendor has ever been in touch with you since you bought it. It's a crowded, polluted, and confused marketplace where price is a major factor simply because there's no other differential. Most users are not motivated to upgrade so most retailers fail to generate repeat sales as there is no clearly identifiable time cycle.

This is the time when you as the salesperson, should be most active in your sales efforts. It doesn't mean the *only* time, though, as you should be reminding your customer that you're still around even when he's not buying.

If your product has a replacement cycle of three years, then the time to start selling again (lead-time) is between three and six months beforehand. Generally, the more expensive the item, the longer the lead-time to purchase becomes.

Of course, if you're smart, you will have been in touch with the customer in the meantime anyway. Having bought a dishwasher from you, it makes sense that they would be predisposed to make their next whitegoods purchase from you. Keeping them in the loop about washing machines, microwaves and fridges would make sense.

What is your customer really buying from you?

Insurance brokers sell insurance, yes; what the customer is really buying is peace of mind. Private schools are selling education, yes; the parents are also buying an educational philosophy, day-care (don't laugh!), and a peer group for their children.

A software package provides the user with the outcome it delivers, not the code in which it was written.

Take a moment now to jot down the answers to the following three questions.

- What benefits does your product deliver?
- Why would someone want to buy it?

- How or why is it unique, desirable, and attractive to the buyer?

When you are calling a prospective customer to arrange a meeting to discuss your product, you need to have something to say that is of interest to the buyer. A request to meet to review their Insurance needs probably won't get you in the door, but a request to meet to review that they have adequate cover to ensure peace of mind may do so.

An attempt to sell seats for a training course probably won't sell the course, but a discussion relating to the consequences of attending the course will, especially when you know the issues within the business.

Who is your buyer?

Answer the following questions on Page 10 of your workbook (jamesyuille.com/WYLTSWorkbook).

- What do you already know about them?
- What are their habits?
- What do they read?
- What else do they own?
- Does your buyer need to have a certain size or structure to be a candidate for your service?
- Do they need to have a minimum turnover or staff size to become your customer?

Unless you sell a product that absolutely everyone wants and needs *(and if you have, please let me know what it is!)*, you need to develop a customer profile to help you focus your selling time on those people/businesses that are most likely to want to buy from you.

You would agree I'm sure, that it is a waste of time trying to sell things to folk who don't want or need them.

Retirement villages don't sell well to under 30's and gaming consoles don't sell well to the over 70's. Fleet vehicle discounts don't apply to companies who have less than a certain number of vehicles. Buyers for $1,000,000-plus properties must have the cash or be able to service the loan.

People who own horses also need feed, tack, clothing and maybe a special trailer to transport their animals to events. If you sold horse floats, you'd be wasting your time promoting them in a dog breeder's magazine whilst ignoring the equestrian publications.

When you visit amazon.com you will see beside each product a list of other items that people who have bought the first item have also bought. The idea here is to get you to buy another item too.

Now, it's time to create your customer profile. That way you know who to focus your best attention and your marketing on first.

Use two criteria for this: grade and timeframe. The grade determines which category of likelihood they fall into. "A" graders are those whose profile closest match my criteria and will be in the market within the next six months. "B" graders either have a lower match or are "A" graders who aren't in the market for at least six months, and so on.

Let me introduce you to the terms, "Back End" and, "Marginal Propensity" as you may not have heard them before.

You'll hear marketers talk about the "Back End" sale. That's the sale you make later *because* you made this one. Here are a couple of simple examples of back end sales...

Let's revisit McDonalds where we've all been and all heard, "Did you want fries with that?" And here's the simple truth: they wouldn't say it if it didn't help them increase the value of the sale. Here's a simple question for you:

A pharmacist once asked himself the, "Did you want fries with that" question. He wanted to know what else he could sell to customers along with whatever they came in to buy. He decided to ask everyone who bought liquid medicines from him if they had a measuring cup to dispense it with. What happened?

Hundreds of people bought a 10-cent measuring cup every month. Many more toothbrushes were sold when people buying toothpaste were asked when they last bought a new toothbrush. These simple questions increased his annual turnover by thousands of dollars.

What is the equivalent question to, "Did you want fries with that?" for your business?

Economists talk about, "Marginal Propensity".

Marginal Propensity examines the options available for the expenditure of an amount of funds. For example, if you have $2,000 available to you, how many ways could you spend it? Perhaps you could spend it on a new refrigerator, on a holiday, or on new clothes? Maybe repairs to your car are a priority?

Just because you advocate a certain solution to a prospect, doesn't mean they'll spend their money that way. There may be twenty different ways that money could be spent. Your recommended solution will only get the nod if it's perceived as the best option; the one that creates the most pleasure or avoids the most pain, and/or the one that makes or saves the prospect the most money.

OK, now we've got that process clear, let's look at what you're selling. Yes, your product or service. I've heard people say that they don't need lots of product knowledge to sell. And that's quite often true. If you sell cars for instance, you don't really need to be able to describe how an automatic gearbox or a fuel injection system works.

The same would apply for the technical aspects of many products. Unless your role is that of a Technical Salesperson in which case, you would need to know. *(And, if you are, and come from a technical background, you need this text because most technical people don't understand the people aspects of selling.)*

Always remember that the most important thing you need to know about your product is what it will do for its intended buyer: your customer.

Next let's look at a SWOT analysis for your service.

SWOT stands for Strengths, Weaknesses, Opportunities and Threats.

Grab a pen and a piece of paper; write down as many answers as you can think of for each of the questions about your business and your offerings. Right now.

Yes, everything.

This is the beginning of the, "Bullet-proofing" process. "Bullet-proofing," means arming you with more than enough information to tackle any question that comes your way.

The Strengths of your business/ product are all the good things about which you can think.

Every neat design aspect, every button, every fact you have available (the good ones, I mean).

Include warranty, testimonials, guarantee, service, availability, price, and colour range.

Detail everything you do well.

Leave nothing out, even if it sounds trivial. That trivial item may just be the difference between making a major sale and not making that sale. They're all relevant.

The Weaknesses are the things about which you hope the customer doesn't ask! The things your competition can do that you can't.

The things that next year's model will be able to do but this year's model can't. Those annoying little problems the service people are *still* trying to fix.

The things that you and your associates realise you need to fix. Detail everything you can improve, everything you avoid and everything you do badly.

Opportunities include all the customer types you haven't yet got to, those untapped territories where you don't have a distributor. Overseas markets. The internet. Include all the design modifications of which you've thought but never incorporated.

Add all the finance options, the direct-mail campaigns you've never tried and the upgrade and on-sell opportunities available by revisiting your existing client database. *(You have got an existing client database, haven't you?)*

Threats are just that. They are the external and internal factors that threaten your success. Don't *just* write about your competition, though. Consider technology or changes in delivery or fulfilment methods, too.

Years ago, when refrigerators were first introduced, my grandmother was concerned about what would happen to the iceman who carried blocks of ice to her home.

The same kind of change is happening today. The internet is one example. It allows immediate transfer of information, rendering many traditional publishing activities potentially obsolete. It allows small companies and individuals to compete with the big end of town.

The Internet is the launch-pad that flattens the world. Google's brilliant advertising platform, AdWords, creates an even more level playing field.

The iceman didn't survive unless he retrained to become a refrigeration mechanic or found something else he could deliver *(like fridges!)*. He forgot he was in the transport business, not the ice business.

Burlington became the major railroad company in the USA because it knew that transport was its business, not railroads.

Many traditional publishers didn't survive the Internet either. Kindle and similar eReaders have changed publishing forever, giving indie authors' exposure and traction as buyers, rather than publishers, decide what they want to buy. Blogs and social media provide authors with viral media platforms thanks to Like and Share functions.

Your business, your product or your service could be threatened, or even worse, made redundant, by new technology developments that you haven't even considered.

Before you decide to leave this until later and rush off to the next section, let me stress the importance of the exercise.

Far too frequently, salespeople don't express the key elements of their product/service in terms that motivate the buyer. Impartial third parties will see things you don't see as you're too close to your own product.

Buyers are often bombarded with information that has no relevance to them. Your buyer will be easily persuaded to your solution if the solution you propose is relevant.

In other words, when the buyers see that it solves their problem. You can't begin to solve a problem you haven't identified.

To solve a problem, you must first know what the problem is. Then you can explain what aspects of your product address the issues. To be able to do this requires you to have a thorough understanding of the strengths of your product.

That's why you need to know all of them. Understanding your opportunities allows you to plan growth and to launch assaults into previously uncharted areas.

Likewise, understanding your weaknesses and threats allows you to build defensive strategies around them.

By now you've learned the TIPS process and you understand the Theory of Consequence. You know your strengths and weaknesses. You're ready to start a new wave of prospecting and marketing.

Remember

ONLY present your product when you're fully aware of the buyers' situation.

Present it by showing how it addresses their problem.

Chapter 9

How to Find Prospects

I expect that you've already begun to use some of the techniques we've looked at over the last few chapters. By now you are thinking consequences; about your questioning techniques, and how to communicate your business to your marketplace.

The Infomercial

Infomercials are also known as, "Elevator Adverts" – the speech you'd give about your product in an elevator ride from the ground to the 30th floor.

Useful in a variety of situations, the Infomercial is your verbal advert. You should have several variants available depending on the circumstances. Use the version best suited to the situation at the time.

Focus on creating 10 and 30-second versions. Use the 10-second version here, and we'll cover where to use the 30-second version in a later chapter.

On many other occasions you will be asked, "What is your business/product/service all about?" Therefore, you need to be prepared. Your answer must appeal to the questioner and must be expressed in an appropriate number of words.

If asked about your business whilst working on a stand at a trade show, unless you can identify the person asking, your answer must be brief, precise, and designed to generate another question.

You may be selling winches for boat trailers. You might say, "We supply winches that make it easier to get your boat out of the water. What sort of trailer do you have?"

If they don't have a trailer (or a boat) they will tell you. You can't sell them unless they want to buy a boat or a trailer, so ask them if they are here to buy one. If not, unless they are a dealer (in which case they will tell you,) don't waste your time.

If you are asked to make a short presentation about your product at the exhibition, identify the audience. If it's people from within the boating industry, talk about the aspects of your winch that will interest them. Design specifications: mean time between failures, service support – all the things that will make it easy for them to sell your product for you.

If the audience is boat owners, tell them how the winch will save them time and effort (gain more pleasure from their boating). Tell them that it's reliable and easy to attach to their current trailer (avoid pain).

Tell them what they want to hear!

By having 10, 30, 60-second and two-minute versions of the story of your product ready to run at any time, you are well placed to answer the question about your product or service effectively and with punch. Remember to do two things before you answer the question:

1. Think about the relationship between the person asking the question and where they fit in relation to the decision-making process.

3. Wait, take a breath, and exhale before answering.

The pause created by taking a breath and exhaling suggests you have thought about their question before answering, allowing you to be certain she's finished asking. She might add something relevant if you give her this small window of silence. The extra information may give you a clue about which of your answers to use.

While working with technology training company Futurekids, we taught their staff to have grabs of information ready to answer the question, "What is Futurekids?" A schoolteacher, a school principal, a school student, a parent, a business owner, an exhibition visitor or even a stranger at a social function may ask the question.

Each justifies a different answer and may need to be variable in length. You may not require as many; develop at least four to start with.

Having four infomercials means you are well prepared when it comes time to introduce your product or service at exhibitions and to introduce yourself to the technical or financial person, the employee, or the decision-maker. Each of these situations requires an answer of varying length.

You've delivered your infomercial. For you to explain how best your service would work for them, you'll need to ask them a few questions about their business, so confirm that it's OK for you to do so.

Chapter 15 details how to create and deliver your infomercials.

Let's now look at prospecting techniques.

How you go about finding people to sell to.

The chances are that you don't have an unlimited amount of new client enquiries. So, if you must prospect for new business, this section is especially for you.

There are several ways to generate new business leads. Let's examine a few of them.

Walk in the door cold calling

This is where you literally walk in through the front door of a prospect's office and ask to see someone about what you sell. Not a commonly used technique these days, but a great way to learn a few essential skills. Please don't look to this method as being the only way to sell because it's not!

Many very successful companies use this method for their sales activities. Cable TV wouldn't exist in many areas unless teams of direct salespeople had knocked on doors. Heaps of roofs would leak if roofing restoration companies hadn't knocked on doors.

A significant number of Real Estate listings result from door knocking, as do votes for political candidates. Phone and energy companies have used doorknocking to get consumers to switch providers for years.

You might find this technique unpalatable; used correctly, it can be very profitable. It's how you do it that's important.

Consider that everyday people like you walk into a potential customer's business premises. They all expect to see someone who will fall in love with their sales pitch and make a buying decision.

Do you really think they have people just sitting around waiting for salespeople to walk in so they can spend their hard-earned money? I didn't think you did!

The person who greets you as you arrive is trained **not** to let you in.

They see this as intrusive marketing or selling by interruption. They see you as a distraction. You're someone to be got rid of, and quickly. However, with the right technique, and by asking the correct questions, you can reasonably expect to establish an appropriate contact with whom to talk and perhaps follow-up with an email.

Here's how it goes - and remember that your mission is to get a name!

Ask if they use your product or service, and if so, whom you might be able to advise of new developments or updates in service.

Make appropriate notes or ask for a card or "With Compliments" slip, thank them for their assistance and leave.

You should consider it a real bonus if you are given the opportunity to see the person right away. It will happen, and you should be ready for it.

Here's where your 10-second infomercial comes in. Use the one appropriate for the person and then follow it up with, "Have you a few minutes now so we can discuss (the benefit)?"

If they say no, arrange a suitable time to meet again, and leave.

Now you have an appointment with someone who is interested enough to fix a time, find out more. That's valuable; well done!

The cold phone call

The main lesson with phone calls is this: You must not try to make a sales presentation over the phone. (This doesn't apply if you're a tele sales person.)

The purpose of the call is to either establish an appropriate contact name or to fix a time to meet.

Introduce yourself first, and then ask for the person by name if you know it. If not, ask who the person might be who would most be interested in (state your benefit).

If you can't get to speak with the right person, a great follow-up question which will save you lots of time in the future is, "That's OK, could you please suggest a time when I'd be likely to catch her in the office?"

This shows you are polite, keen, and not going to keep on calling aimlessly. Please do not try to do any more than this over the phone!

If you get to talk with the right person, simply use one of your consequence statements and say,

"Mrs. Johnson, I'm Tom Simons of XYZ Company. Our customers find that we are very good at (service).

"Would you be available for a discussion about how (consequence of service) could work for you?"

Phrased correctly, this approach will open doors for you.

You will need a fall-back point. Not everyone will give a positive response.

Have a mailing piece or website URL available as a follow-up and have the person agree to let you call her soon.

Google Ads

I'm a huge fan of Google's Advertising platforms and a significant portion of our revenue today comes from the training and consulting work we do with this media. For more information about Google advertising, visit mediaglue.com.au/ads

Most people think of AdWords as being the text ads you see on Google's search results pages (known as Search Advertising). Yet this media extends way beyond that with their Display (advertising on other people's websites), YouTube, Shopping (where products from your shopping cart are displayed on the Search results page for you to buy direct), App download promotion and Remarketing options.

Search Advertising is where most people start. Generally, your product should be worth over $250 and have at least one of the following:

- High profit
- High likelihood of repeat sales
- A more valuable backend or upsell

The major advantage Search Advertising with Google Ads has over social media advertising platforms is that your ads show when people search for what you do. It's pure direct response marketing.

Combined with Remarketing and Display campaigns, Search advertising can be highly effective. We have a wide range of clients who use Google Ads as their prime lead generation source. Some must pause their campaigns from time-to-time due to too much work coming in. For most, Google Ads provides a reliable stream of incoming enquiries providing them with a stable and scalable platform for growth.

The referral

These are like liquid gold. Let me tell you, no matter how good you get at this selling business, referrals are still fantastic!

Here's how to handle them. Call the person to whom you've been referred and as always, introduce yourself to the phone guardian.

Be careful over the benefit you choose to lead with (ask the referrer), and then say, "I've been asked to call Mr. Brown by Mrs. Black of XYZ Fastenings. Is he available, please?"

Only if necessary, you can add, "Mrs. Black thought Mr. Brown would be interested to hear how we saved them money and time in their packaging department."

If Mr. Brown knows Mrs. Black and respects her judgment, this will work for you. Even better, ask Mrs. Black to call Mr. Brown for you, or persuade her to write an introductory letter or email for you.

Testimonial letters are very handy, and we'll talk about them in a later chapter, along with how to use referral programs as a lead-generating method.

The incoming enquiry call

This is where most people screw up! How many times do incoming callers ask you, "How much is your Mk 3 widget?" or worse still, "What's your best price for a Mk 3?"

Here's an interesting position to take:

The only time in your life you're *compelled* to answer the question that is asked is when you're under oath in Court.

You will not find the statement, "Thou shalt answer the question asked in a direct manner" in any book on sales, negotiation, or human behaviour.

I'm **not** advocating that you tell an untruth. I am suggesting that you should consider the motivation for the question before answering it and that you look to take control of the conversation.

For instance, if the question was, "How much is your Mk 3 widget?" you answer with questions like this:

"Yes, I can help you with that, and for me to best assist, I'd like to check a couple of things with you first.

"What is it about the Mk 3 that interests you?"

Let them answer. That will help you make sure the Mk 3 is the one they need. If it's not, discuss the options by asking more questions. Once you've identified the right model, ask something like this...

"Tell me how many Mk 3's you'd be looking for, and how often you need them?"

Answering a question with a question helps you regain control of the conversation.

I'm not advocating that you become aggressive though; simply reminding you that you lose control if you're doing all the answering.

It's very unusual if, when you answer a question with a question, to get a third question in response. If you do, be alert – you have a good negotiator on your hands.

If you have any doubt about the accuracy of this observation, engage yourself in a conversation with a young child. He or she will ask you question after question, even if you ask one back. Instinctively, children know that they need to control the conversation, and do so with this technique.

If you have a half-genuine buyer on your hands, you should start to participate in a conversation about individual buying needs.

A young lady got a new job, was given a desk and a phone, and told her role was to help callers with their enquiries. That month she topped the sales charts. Overwhelmed by the plaudits and not realising she was actually *selling* – she thought the role was merely to assist people -- her figures fell. She was now frightened to give the appropriate advice as she didn't want to be seen to be *selling* something!

Establish the amount, frequency, current supplier, and their real use for the product.

Establish that the Mk 3 is the best widget for them. They might not have heard about your Mk 4 or the Super Series 2 widget! Why do they want Widgets anyway? What do they make with them?

By now, you are starting to gain the caller's trust. Your company isn't in business just to quote prices over the phone. You are there to provide a quality service to users of widgets, underpinned by professional advice and back-up support.

Your buyer may be dealing with your arch-rival, ACE widgets that has let their customer down. He or she may have been faced with an out-of-stock situation with ACE and is desperate to keep the production-line going.

The point is that unless you ask the questions, you're never going to know. If you don't know the reason for the call, how do you expect to get the business? It would be by sheer luck that had you answered, "The Mk 3 is $23.65" your caller would have replied, "OK, my order number is 4538H, I'll have 300 please"

(You and I both know that doesn't happen, don't we?)

You must establish how every incoming caller found out about you and what you do. Apart from helping you steer the call, it's vital for monitoring the effectiveness of your marketing. A great line to use early in the conversation is, "What prompts your call?"

I must tell you a little story here. I took an unexpected call from someone who had bought an earlier version of this book. His opening words were, "James this is *(name protected)* and I hate you!"

Shocked, I asked him why he held such strong feelings. My exact words were, "Thanks, what prompts you to say that?"

"I read your recommendation to ask, 'What prompts your call?' and kicked myself for not thinking of it first. I own several businesses and immediately scheduled a sales meeting for all my people for the next day. I explained how to use that phrase and over the next week, our sales increased by 15%. I hate you simply because I wish I'd known that phrase years ago, but now want to thank you for the result it generated."

You may be offering a professional service such as legal services, accountancy or financial planning. Whilst at face value, the process may appear different; in fact, it's the same.

Your goal is to secure a face-to-face meeting or agree to a fee-for-service engagement. Most professional service providers operate within a small geographic area – we don't generally hire an accountant in Glasgow if we live in Southampton or a lawyer in New Orleans if we live in Boston or a solicitor in Toowoomba if we live in Sydney.

The client generally seeks you out because they've seen your sign or an advert or found you by using a search engine. *(Tip: tagging your website with your location, using Google Business, or using location-specific pay-per-click ads all really work)*

They are calling you because they have a problem or need help.
They don't ring just to chat!

It's probable that you don't take the calls yourself; after all, you're too busy, so you have an assistant, a paralegal, an office manager or business development person take the call.

Here's what to do:

Train your people in what to say. Many businesses allow the lowest-paid, least-skilled, least-motivated person to take the most important call; the new client enquiry.

Unfortunately, what can happen is that staff deviate from the script and despite you telling them what they want to have happen, the staff member ends up doing what he or she wants. If this is you, it's imperative that you stand your ground and make the rules stick.

The task of the person answering the phone or responding to the enquiry email is to secure a meeting, a fee-for-service call or to get a name so you can call back or mail something to them. Ensure your staff uses the, "Tell–me-about" process, identifies why the caller is calling and what the caller expects from the transaction.

Anything less is a failure.

In a recent training session with a law firm, introducing the, "Tell–me-about" questioning process increased the conversion rate of callers to first consultations by 25%. The consequence of seeing more people face-to-face was, of course, more new clients.

New clients equal extra dollars in the door.

The task for the lawyer when they met was to identify the exact problem and explain how he could solve it for them.

The incoming direct marketing response

Ideally, calls generated by a marketing campaign should be directed to an appropriate number so that they are easily identified. This isn't always possible, so if it's not, the campaign should have the caller requesting a special offer or department (look at direct- response adverts that say to quote Department J when calling.) Calls from direct campaigns are mainly of three kinds:

- Requests for more information (e.g. a catalogue or a free consultation)
- To arrange to meet
- To make a purchase

Being prepared with appropriate responses is the key to generating sales from your marketing campaign.

Recall our earlier discussion about increasing your turnover by over 30%. The first step was to increase your conversion rate by 10%. This way, even if you didn't manage to increase the value of the sale by 10%, you'd still have a 10% lift without additional work or expense.

You can see how easy it is to increase the numbers of people you get to talk to just by asking the right questions at the enquiry stage. Now consider that if you're getting to see 10 or 15% more people, converting an extra 10% overall can be relatively easy.

When a potential customer phones, emails, visits your website or walks into your store, what's the single most important thing to do?

The most important thing you can do is get their name and a way to keep in touch; usually a phone number or email address. This is one of the prime reasons why there are so many loyalty programs popping up – who doesn't want points on their purchase or a voucher on their birthday?

Unless you have their name, you can't stay in touch with them. Because people don't generally buy on their first visit, they usually need convincing.

And if you don't have their name, how can you get back to them?

Here's the first part of the strategy: establish a process to get your visitor's name. There are lots of ways to do this. Here are a few...

- Run a contest where you give away something of value every month just for visiting the store. In men's clothing for instance, you could give away quality ties or quality polo shirts.
- Invite them to join your mailing list to get advance information on new releases and specials.
- Tell them about your loyalty program and explain that even though they're not yet customers, the benefits apply.

Not sure how a loyalty program could work for you? Here are a few examples:

Coffee Cards. There are several types.

Bring a friend; buy one and get one free

Buy a certain number and get the next free

Pre-pay a certain number and a discount up front. This acts like a gift card; over 10% of gift cards are never fully redeemed, making easy money for the retailer.

Ladies hairdressing. Explain to your customers that advertising is expensive and rather than spend hundreds on newspaper adverts, you'd rather spend that money on your clients. Give them a few cards introducing the salon to their friends, offering a free treatment, preferably a service they would not otherwise have considered.

When the client has introduced three friends who each have visited four times, give the original client a stylish gift basket or a meal voucher for two at a quality restaurant.

Car maintenance. Provide credit points for extra services for each scheduled maintenance visit. Credits could be used for minor scratch and dent repairs, wheel alignments, etc.

Restaurants. When taking a call about booking a table, unless the voice and/or name is already familiar to you, say this; 'You've dined with us before haven't you?' If the response is, 'yes' say, 'I thought so, it will be nice to have you here again' and note next to the booking that the person is a return customer.

If not, say this, 'That's fantastic, I'll make sure we explain our new customer specials when you arrive.' This may be a free drink, half-priced entrée; something to welcome them.

As they leave, give them a voucher to return with friends saying their friends will receive a similar benefit.

This has been tested and proven very effective.

Once you have their name recorded, and permission to use it to send them information (necessary where privacy laws exist to stop "SPAM" marketing), you need a follow-up program.

Develop a plan and make sure you follow it up. Depending on what business you're in, this may be solely direct mail, a combination of mail (don't discount sending letters; when was the last time you got one?), phone (yes, people still like to talk), visits or email.

You need to store these names in a database of some form to enable you to merge details such as names and addresses into your letters and automate your marketing campaigns.

If you have a website, use what we call an, 'Ethical Bribe.' This involves providing useful information in exchange for their name and email address.

We ran a promotion for a construction company who had previously sold via display homes. This was about the time the GFC hit in 2008. We encouraged them to sell off their display homes and instead, focus on Internet advertising. Reluctant at first; as their sales were falling, they agreed to proceed.

A new website was quickly launched with an offer to receive a free, full-colour book of house designs in return for their name and address (for postage) along with the location of the land on which they planned to build. Without this information, they could not get the book.

They sold their display homes which also meant four very bored and uninterested salespeople resigned. The online advertising campaign kicked in and within three months they were selling more homes than when they relied on newspaper ads and display homes.

A wedding DJ wrote a little booklet about wedding reception do's and don'ts. Using his experience, the order of events, tips for the Master of Ceremonies, speeches, and general protocols were set out. A few horror stories of how things can go wrong with an amateur DJ or family member, the booklet's job was to secure the writer as the obvious choice.

Another one we ran was to promote the use of rainwater tanks in domestic environments. It was again launched through Google AdWords

Use your mailing/email broadcasts to further develop your prospective customer's trust. Webinars and videos are equally useful tools.

Email broadcasts are the easiest and cheapest by far. You can either send a sequence of pre-programmed messages or forward a regular newsletter to your database.

Use a professional autoresponder program such as Mailchimp®. Using Outlook or Gmail to do your broadcasts doesn't cut it with today's anti-SPAM legislation. You want one with flat, fixed costs too. One client found out that he was spending over $300 every time he sent out his newsletter. *Ouch.*

An autoresponder lets you send personalised emails to your suspects, prospects and customers alike, around the world, at the click of your mouse. Remember that it's not the number of people on your list that matters. The best lists are those with names of people who have chosen to be there as they have an interest in doing business with you.

With or without a website, an autoresponder can make you money by delivering a timely message about you and your business straight to the prospective customer's inbox.

Make sure you comply with anti-SPAM legislation by providing a documented method of unsubscribing. The best autoresponders have a single click, 'Unsubscribe' function.

I also encourage you to keep a record of the number of enquiries you receive, the results you gain from each advert or promotion you undertake, and every publication in which you run them.

There are only three possible results: Sold, lost to a competitor, or decided not to buy.

You should track your results because this is a solid indicator of your improving performance. Every competent salesperson should track the conversion rate. It will also give you an indication of your ROI on advertising expenditure, and if this increases or decreases over time.

How to develop your marketing campaigns to create enquiries is discussed later.

Remember

The most desirable outcome of the prospecting process is for you to get their name and a way of contacting them.

If you can't sell them immediately, you can stay in touch with them and develop a relationship.

You can't measure what you can't record.

Chapter 10

Consultative Selling

Put yourself in your customers' shoes and image yourself sitting on their side of the table looking at the issue from where they sit.

You are not there to sell them; you are there to remove their pain, to solve their problem or challenge, or to present an opportunity.

Now what? Where do your go from here?

Your goal is to have the buying process start as early and as quickly as possible by making the irresistible offer.

Your offer becomes irresistible when it clearly solves your prospective customer's problem and is as close to risk-free as you can possibly make it.

With high trust, a clearly identified solution and low risk to risk-free entry, your job is complete. High trust equals relationships which equals money. R=M.

Here's how to start getting there in the shortest possible timeframe.

We've looked at Trust. It revolves around the way you make your approach, the way you look, the way you start the conversation with appropriate questions, and the way you respond to the answers you get.

I'm often asked how you know when to end the small talk and get down to business and it's a hard one to answer directly. It's like asking when the dog is going to bite. All I can say is that as you gain more experience, you'll know. It's that unconscious competence thing again.

You certainly can't just start with the business issues. There's need for an icebreaker of some kind. Again, I can't tell you what to say; you will just have to trust your intuition. For men, that can be difficult; we're not used to trusting our intuition. For women, well, it's easier. You know how to judge this.

All I can say is that if you are tuned in to the conversation with your buyer, you will instinctively know when the time comes. Sometimes it's seconds into the conversation and at other times, it can be half an hour. You have to learn to judge this for yourself. I can't teach you.

If you're struggling with a conversation starter, I suggest you should keep your eyes and ears open to the environment you experience when you first visit your buyer.

Look for awards hanging on the wall, glance through the magazines while waiting in the reception area for articles about the company or industry.

Recall news items about the industry (reading a daily newspaper has helped me with conversation starters many, many times) or even remark about the family photo on the desk.

If the photo has children or pets in it, and you are a parent, talk about children. Your goal is to get the buyer involved in a conversation before you start to talk business.

There's an opportunity in every conversation to strike a common chord that increases trust.

Here's an example…

I was in Los Angeles working with David Newington when he was with FCM Travel. *(You will remember David from earlier in the book, he was my first ever sales coaching client.)* We went on a call together and met with a prospect who mentioned he was going on a trip to China followed by a vacation to Las Vegas.

The call wasn't going terribly well. David was struggling to make headway. Beforehand I had asked David if I could take over if I saw an opportunity he had missed. He agreed.

Here was my moment…

Figuring he would have a reason for visiting Vegas, I asked why he was going.

"To play in a pool tournament," he replied.

David is a very keen snooker player. He played competitively in Australia before heading to LA and hadn't become involved with the game since arriving. The conversation was righted and assumed a more natural flow as we talked about pool and snooker.

The client turned out to be a member of the Hollywood Snooker Club and, you guessed it; David was living in Hollywood at the time. His relationship with that client was cemented by that one question.

It is often a good idea to explore their world. You do that by asking questions. Probe until you find something interesting, something relevant and take it wherever it needs to go.

I've generally found it necessary to start the business part of the conversation with one of my "infomercials" so that the buyer is refreshed about the reason for my visit. It may well be that the meeting was scheduled some weeks beforehand, and the reason for your visit is no longer front of mind.

(Don't laugh – this has happened to me on more than one occasion. I once spent an hour with a buyer before we established that I wasn't from the company he thought I was from, even though he'd seen my business card!)

You might start by delivering your short "infomercial" - remembering we covered this earlier - and then adding that you'd like to ask a few questions about how they do/go about certain related activities in their business.

We're now into the 'I' stage

Identifying is about listening to the responses given to your questions.

This is where you must be attentive and canny. Somewhere in the conversation, you will pick up the vital clues) that you need to complete this transaction. It may be a comment about how the current supplier has let them down. It may be about a problem that they have meeting a customer's delivery requirements.

Whatever it is, you need to be listening. You also need to be ready with the next question, too. That's why you must be prepared.

You can't be thinking about your next question while they're answering the last one. If you are, you'll miss the very gem you need to go on. It's like prospecting for precious stones. Don't ignore the opals whilst scouring for diamonds!

Proposing an appropriate solution is when you identify with the problem and start recommending solutions. You are now showing the customer how to gain pleasure or avoid pain or make or save money or time. This is where your consequence statements are going to be best used.

Now you are becoming an advocate for your solution, and unless the person with whom you are speaking is the ultimate decision-maker, your role is to ensure he becomes an advocate for your solution, too. Unless he is that person, he won't adequately represent you at the higher level.

The ideal situation is of course, for you to be talking directly to the decision-maker. This isn't always possible, and so your advocate needs to be so totally convinced about your solution that if something goes wrong with the process, this person will come back to you and discuss another approach.

This can be likened to the situation where you want to buy something and must convince your husband or wife that it's a good idea. You become the salesperson's advocate in the sale, and you get to hear all the obstacles.

If you've been properly bullet-proofed, the result you want will happen. If not, it won't. Your advocate in the client relationship is in the same position when selling your solution to his or her superiors.

I had one just like this very recently.

Dealing with a large client, I couldn't reach the final decision-maker. Brian (my advocate) and I discussed a solution to the problem we had identified, and my proposal was delivered to the management team.

Unfortunately, they didn't like the implementation plan upon which Brian, and I had agreed, and rejected the proposal. Brian emailed me immediately and explained what had happened. We met again and redesigned the package, incorporating a different implementation strategy.

The resubmitted proposal was approved.

Note that it was my proposed solution they didn't accept, not my diagnosis of the problem. Because my advocate wanted me to deliver the solution, he gave me the opportunity to repackage the proposal.

Because I had taken time to develop a great rapport with him, he told me how I had to repackage my offer to meet their needs. It worked out well. My second offer was both more expensive and more profitable for me. Talk about win – win.

This illustrates that if your advocate is totally convinced that your solution will work, your proposal will be supported, and you will have the opportunity to renegotiate if things go wrong.

Now you have a series of feature – function – benefit – consequence statements about your product. Let's look at how to use them.

Features, you will remember, are the facts. Facts appeal to engineers, statisticians, accountants, and the like. You especially need to use features when proposing your solution to these buyers.

Functions are generally used to explain features to non-technical people. A not-so-technical person appreciates you adding, "that means it has a large memory and runs very fast."

The benefits are that it will hold all the software they need and that files will open and run quickly.

The consequences are that the machine won't need to be upgraded for quite some time and that no time will be lost waiting for the machine to boot up. This will appeal to both the financial person and to the final decision-maker (the boss) who wants to know that the investment will have safe, long-term ramifications (in this case, no more to spend).

Learn how, when and where to use these statements, and in what combination.

You will learn this by listening to the problems unveil as you ask your newly discovered open and tell-me-about questions. You will then use the appropriate selection of feature – function – benefit – consequence to advocate your solution.

By strongly advocating the consequences that address the time/money issue, you are painting a picture of urgency and accelerating the timeline.

I know you're thinking, "It's not as easy as that" and you're right. You can't always get to the exact person who makes the decisions. Where there's a committee or board involved advocating your solution may appear impossible. Here's where having identified the problem and proposed the appropriate solution to your contact, your extra efforts will return dividends.

On many occasions, you must let someone else do the selling for you. Remember the last two questions I gave you earlier, about how to identify if you are dealing with the real decision-maker? Therefore you need to ask!

When you're unable to directly influence the decision-maker, the person you can influence has to become your advocate. By supplying this individual with enough ammunition and protection (information and answers), that person will do the job for you. That's why you must recognise that you can't sell to everyone.

The final point is, **Setting** a timeline. Again, this can be tricky, but the key lies in the identification process. If you've accurately identified or diagnosed the problem, then by using the correct consequence statements, you will have created your own sense of urgency.

If the solution involves a financial saving, then your approach will be along the lines of *"How long do you want to wait before you enjoy these savings?"*

If it involves pleasure, the lines to follow are those that pursue the enjoyment of the benefit. The pleasure benefit of a swimming pool is much easier to sell in spring than autumn; however, the cost-saving of construction during winter is easier to sell in autumn.

This is about pushing the buyer's hot buttons. You can do this successfully only after you've established the real motivations for the buying decision.

If my real motive for buying a car is that I have a child on the way and I have a two-seater, my hot buttons are, having a vehicle in time to bring the baby home from hospital, about safety and convenience. Depending upon the stage of the pregnancy, I may only have a very short time to decide.

Likewise, if you are selling painting and decorating and the room you're being asked to quote on is a baby's bedroom, you have an urgency opportunity too.

You should know the reason for their purchase, as unless you do, you can't use urgency effectively.

You won't know how to introduce a sense of urgency if you haven't correctly identified the problem or the reason for making the purchase. Once you have, it's a cinch.

While we're on the subject of the four steps, let me make one more very important point. Unless you complete each one of these in order, you can't successfully expect to move along to the next.

Liken it to climbing a ladder with the rungs widely spaced. It just isn't practical for you to get straight from the first step to the third. Look back at sales you've not completed, and review them with this question:

Which step did I successfully reach?

Unless all this is going extremely well, you are likely to get the odd obstacle thrown in your way. Many sales trainers call these obstacles, "objections". It's another term I dislike, so if it's OK with you, we'll call them "obstacles" because obstacles are things you can climb over or drive around.

There have been many theories promoted about handling these obstacles. One manual I read described a five-point approach with a pitch so ridiculous that I laughed aloud when reading it. It was ridiculous to the point of embarrassment. Typically, you might get asked things like:

- Do you have them in blue?
- Can I get it by next Friday?
- Will you be able to fit it here?

This kind of obstacle is easily answered. The response is, "Did you particularly want blue/Friday delivery (or whatever)". If the answer is, 'yes,' then you can correctly assume that the transaction is going your way. You may well be able to complete the transaction by asking a confirmation question such as, "Would you prefer delivery on Friday, or would earlier in the week be better?" An appropriate answer confirms completion.

The third one, "Will it fit", is best answered with, "We'd better measure it up." If the answer is, 'yes' again, you're on track. If the answer is, 'no', you need to backtrack to find common ground again. Sometimes the buyer will ask you an irrelevant question.

They do it to test you out, to establish how focused you are, or just to be awkward. It may be that they are curious and sometimes it's good to check just why the question was asked.

You may give a very short answer and add, "Does that answer the question, or did you need more detailed information?" If they genuinely need more details, ask precisely what they need and why they need it and either give it to them or agree to come back with it.

Some obstacles require more effort to circumvent. When they are put in your way, ponder the question for a moment, asking yourself why they are asking it and where you have missed the signal that it was an issue. Respond accordingly with the necessary information, check that you've covered the topic and move on.

Sometimes, a question comes right out of left field. One you've not heard before, or just seems irrational.

Sometimes your competitor, who either knows of or at least perceives a weakness in your offering, plants the obstacle. The easiest way to deal with this is to reply to the question or statement with a question like this, "Hmm, that's an interesting question, do you mind me enquiring what prompted you to ask it?"

Don't be surprised what comes back at you and don't be in a hurry to respond. Remember, you've been caught by the question so consider your response.

Remember – you can't and won't win them all!
The key is to examine each obstacle in its own light. Ponder the question, work out what you've missed and go in again. The worksheet at the end of this chapter will give you an opportunity to examine some obstacles that you may have encountered.

Often, you will be asked to provide a proposal about your solution. Before you do, it's important to identify why the proposal is needed. The reason may be that the financial department needs something in writing to enable your invoice to be paid, or that they will be using an external financier to fund the proposal. You will need to provide details to support their loan application.

It may be that your advocate needs to have your proposal outlined in detail so that the members of the relevant authorising committee can read it and understand the idea.

Or it could be a nice way of saying, 'no.'

I developed a line to handle this. It goes like this:

"There are many reasons why different organisations require a written proposal. Some need one for financial or approval purposes and sometimes they're needed as a record of what was agreed. Could I ask you which of these reasons applies this time so I can make sure it's worded appropriately?"

This question generally flushes out the reason and allows me to write the correct letter

About letters, a frequently asked question is, "Do you advocate a personalised proposal, or something generic?" My response is that it depends upon several factors, including the value of the transaction, how customised the solution may be and for what reason the proposal is required.

Here's where your word processor and your database are so useful. They let you have a set of generic letters and proposals pre-prepared to cater for most situations. Just open the most appropriate letter and adjust it to suit the requirement. Similarly, your emailing list will let you send hundreds of promotional emails to your database quickly and for virtually no cost.

The next challenge you face is asking them to buy. I would expect that if you've done everything right, by now your buyer has almost told you that they want to complete the transaction. Your proposed solution should have been given the green light and the next step is to stop selling and move into completion mode.

This is where you start the order-fulfilment process. When you start to complete your paperwork, arrange meetings with support staff, schedule manufacturing timelines or whatever is necessary to get the order to the stage of invoice and payment.

These are all timeline agreements. They form the '**S**' part of TIPS.

Sometimes, though, our buyer isn't telling us that all is clear. We may need to give the person a little prod along the way. This is what the traditional sales training systems call, "the trial close". It's when you ask a simple question that confirms that you're on track and the buyer is still with you. Questions like,

"Let me just recap what we're doing in this room, Ms. George; was it blue walls with white window frames?"

"Do you think this size would fit in your kitchen, Mrs. Marshall?"

"Is this along the lines of what you had in mind, Harry?"

When a positive response is given, you can be safe to assume all is going smoothly. If not, you need to backtrack and find out where you made a false assumption. It may be that you need to ask why they gave that response if they don't agree with you.

I've used the line, "I've obviously missed something along the way here! Could we just go back a step for me to pick up the thread? Now, didn't you say that...?"

Make sure it is phrased in your words; your tone; your style. Don't read this manual as a script because it doesn't work like that. Use my phrases to get used to the concept, but you must make them fit your conversational style.

Once you have passed this little checkpoint, you have the all-clear to move along to what we trust will be the final stage of the sale. The stage when they ask you how they go about procuring what you have proposed to them.

This is like listening to the coins billowing over the tray of a slot machine! It's the Profit Point; it's where you make your money!

If you're reading this and aren't used to selling, let me tell you, the first time a buyer asks how they go about buying from you and asks where they sign, or get out their wallet, your heart will miss a beat.

Stay calm- it certainly won't be the last time and it's why we old hands stay in sales for so long. The feeling of satisfaction is amazing.

Be proud of yourself

You've delivered a solution to their problem. They've agreed that it's viable and want to take your advice.

The most important thing to do now is to stop selling. Switch *immediately* to fulfilment mode. Clear up the small details. These could include the colour and the payment and delivery terms.

"OK Primrose, so you want the wagon with automatic transmission, air-conditioning and a tow-bar. Did you decide if silver or the navy would look best?"

"Did you want to take advantage of the 5% discount for up-front payment, or shall we bill you 30 days?"

"Shall we deliver, or did you want to collect it?"

There are lots of other techniques you can use to confirm their timeline. In some markets, an 'impending event' works well.

A client of mine released a new corporate training manual. It was to have a market price of $990 but for the weeks leading up to release, they offered it at $770 on the basis that intending purchasers would get it immediately upon release. They booked over $16,000 in orders before the product was even out there! How did they sell it?

They used a free sample. They took a completed section of the publication, along with a detailed synopsis of the finished product to several potential buyers and left the sample with them for a week (just like the pet shop letting your 8-year-old take a puppy home for the weekend). 90% of the people who reviewed the sample ordered.

What that also proved to my client was that the material was indeed worth putting the effort into finishing. Within three days of release they had sold another five copies at full price! That's almost $21,000 in invoiced sales inside three days of release. What a great story for their salespeople to tell other potential buyers.

Let's take a moment to reflect on the decision-making process for a minute. For most of us, making decisions doesn't come easily. Consider how long it takes you to make a choice from a menu even when there are only six or eight dishes from which to choose.

Your role as the salesperson is to assist their decision, not to make it for them. That's manipulation and you will suffer from the ignominy of cancelled orders if you make the decision. Don't do it! You will ultimately pay the biggest price of all – you'll lose your job.

Not only that, but under several authorities throughout the world, you will find yourself having to justify your position to some form of Governmental Consumer Protection Agency. These guys bite and with good reason.

They're there to protect us as consumers, and to protect you as an ethical sale's professional.

Follow up

Not every sale is made on the first contact. If your buyer doesn't reach a decision today, there are two possible negative consequences. They decide either not to buy or to buy elsewhere.

We can significantly learn from these negative outcomes by following up.

Keeping in touch by phone, mail, or email, you can stay in tune with their buying process. As a rule of thumb, you should instigate a series of at least seven follow-ups or "touches" with a new prospect.

If your salespeople don't have time to follow up, you must put alternative follow-up processes in place. Use tele sales, direct-mail letters, newsletters, social media etc. All of these, however, can be expensive and time-consuming to initiate and continue.

Or, more easily, you could use an email autoresponder.

Remember This Process

- Identify someone who might want what you sell and get together,
- Establish yourself as a viable supplier.
- Ask questions to confirm that they can use what you sell.
- Explain how your solution will work for them.
- Check that they can decide and can pay for it.
- Agree to a timeline for the transaction to take place.
- Agree to payment terms. (I'd prefer to do that after agreeing to the timeline. There is an emotional fear of loss we can use to our advantage here.)
- If they don't buy first time, follow up.
- If they don't buy at all, read the next chapter to find out why.

Chapter 11

Why People Buy, and Why They Don't

You'll recall when I said that people make decisions based on gaining pleasure or avoiding pain. If we were expanding pleasure and pain into a more detailed list, it might look like this:

1. Make money
2. Save money
3. Save time
4. Avoid effort
5. Increase comfort
6. Improve health
7. Escape physical pain
8. Avoid emotional distress
9. Romance
10. Gain praise
11. Be popular
12. Gain more control

Remember, the purchase decision is made from an emotional position and supported by logic. It's rarely made the other way around.

When you fully understand the emotional consequences of your product, you'll be able to match the consequence to their precise motivation.

There are four key reasons why someone doesn't buy from you:

- They don't want it
- They haven't the authority to buy it
- They can't afford it or can buy it elsewhere for less
- They don't trust you, your company, or your solution

Taking them one at a time, here's how you interpret them.

They don't want it

How did you pick them as a prospect in the first place? You certainly shouldn't be wasting your time trying to sell to someone who isn't a prospect.

Did they call you? If they did, it's your responsibility to identify the reason why they called you. If they're not a prospect, make sure they know as quickly as possible to clear the phone line for someone who is.

If you're calling them, and they say they don't want it, believe them. You won't win by trying to argue that they do want it.

Find someone who does and talk to him or her, instead.

They haven't the authority to buy it

Basically, you're trying to sell to the wrong person. Again, this is your fault. You can't get a decision from someone who hasn't the authority to make one.

Instead, identify the decision-making process within that organisation (or family) and enlist this person as your advocate. By arming him or her with enough ammunition, that individual will then assist you by influencing the key players.

They can't afford it or can buy elsewhere for less

At face value, this appears to be a case of not having the capacity to pay. It's worthwhile to let them know in the first place what the money aspect is likely to represent. You don't buy a new Ferrari on a Kia budget.

Your positioning generally indicates your price. There isn't a Wal-Mart in Rodeo Drive.

Often, the money issue will come up. Classic lines such as, "It's not in our budget" or, "We can't afford it" will be thrown at you.

The prospect genuinely can't afford the solution. It may be way beyond budget (in which case you didn't **identify** correctly), or it may be that it needs to be a budgeted item for expenditure to be approved in the future.

On many occasions this is quite genuine.

It requires you to confirm that the amount will be included in the next budget, and an agreement that you and the buyer will work together to implement the solution as soon as the new budget will allow.

This is often the case with large companies, schools and government organisations.

Having a time-payment or deferred-payment option can help you here.

It may be that you have failed to illustrate the savings your proposal will create. If this is the case, you will need to go over the financial aspects of the solution again and identify how and when the savings may be enjoyed.

Sometimes, they simply can't think of another way to say 'no' to you!

Again, this is a failure in identification or benefit-consequence. Go back or if all is lost, quit the transaction.

A word of caution here: **money is often used as an excuse when there's nothing else to consider.** This is generally revealed when your customer says that he can buy the same thing elsewhere for less.

When you hear this, it's generally because you haven't painted yourself or your company as an essential part of the solution.

You need to consider your warranty/guarantee, service offering, or how you've bundled your offer in terms of support materials.

I recall a conversation with the owner of a bike store. He complained about other stores being cheaper and that he needed to discount as a result. This guy is a serious bike rider having won titles on machines he designed and built himself.

The solution was simple. We looked at what bike buyers bought along with their bikes. He now bundles helmets, drink bottles and gloves in with the bike.

He has added a complimentary, three-month maintenance check where he adjusts the brakes and gears; he offers courses in bike maintenance, and every week he organises several enthusiast rides starting from his shop. He now has a point of difference over the discount and price is no longer an issue

More on establishing your point of difference in Chapter 12.

They don't trust you, your company, or your solution
Did you take the time to establish trust?

Did you discuss testimonials, case studies, and your track record? Were you dressed appropriately?

Was your business card thin and flimsy with a homemade look? (Remember again, you only get one chance to make a first impression. Do it well.)

They doubted that you could be of assistance and didn't reveal their real issues to you as a result.

Your questioning process seemed like an interrogation.

You didn't identify any degree of urgency. It's essential to reach agreement on a timeline for implementing your solution.

Your offer didn't meet their needs; solve their problem; take away pain or provide pleasure. Rethink your offer.

Remember

Think back on every sale you're missed recently.

The reason they didn't buy is probably hiding in the last few pages.

Chapter 12

What to Do Now the Sale Is Made

Hey, it all worked! You now have a new customer; one I hope you wouldn't have had unless you'd put all the steps you've learned so far into place. You have some unique knowledge about this customer too.

You know more about his or her buying motives than you ever did before.

You know *why* they bought from you.

You also know more about their problems than you would have known before. You know more about what you can sell them next. You also have more knowledge about the problem they had so you are better equipped to address it the next time you face it.

Additionally, there are several things you should have done with this information by now. As soon as you contacted this new customer, you should have started to create a database about that person.

If you're in retail, this information may not have started until you made the sale and recorded their name and other details for delivery or for your membership club or for whatever you call your database collection method.

I hope though, that their name came into the conversation earlier and that you used it during the conversation. Most people are more relaxed with someone whose name they know. So wear a name-badge and people will know yours.

The new customer is by far the hardest and most expensive to gain. It's far easier to sell to someone who has bought from you before.

This is because trust has already been established. You know a little more about their likes, preferences, colour tastes, size, etc. Armed with this information you can build solid, regular customers.

In Brisbane, a men's clothing store from which I bought a suit years ago continued to mail me with personalised information about sales and special promotions for several years. And because they sent me information, I went back and bought from them. You see; the owner of the store realises the lifetime value of a customer. Today they would email me.

Look at a typical customer buying apparel from the same store over five years. If he bought one suit every two years, a pair of trousers and a jacket on the alternate years, along with shirts and ties with each purchase, he would have spent over $5,000 in five years. Yet the first sale may have been as little as a couple of hundred dollars.

Because the shop owner understood the concept of "lifelong value", that customer spent up to 50 times more than on the first sale. And the cost of the extra $4,800 in sales? Two mailings each year at say, $5 each for a total of $50.00. Not a bad investment to convert a $100 customer into a $5,000 customer.

Marketers refer to the "back-end sale". I mentioned this term earlier, in case you don't fully understand it, here's an explanation. It refers to the sales you **make** *because of* the sale you **made**.

In the clothing store example, the additional (back-end) sales were worth $4,800.

The backend sale is your prime objective when the first sale is at low cost or low margin..

Here's another example. You attend a two-hour seminar for $25.00. At that seminar, you gain some valuable information that makes spending the $25 worthwhile.

You become aware that the real purpose of the $25 seminar is to sell you a three-day course at $1,500, or a series of books, audios, and videos worth a similar amount. If you don't go to the three-day course, you might make a small investment in a single webinar or book.

You can be guaranteed that over the next twelve months (at least) you will receive offers to attend the three-day course again and again. If you do attend the three-day course, you will also get the opportunity to buy the videos and books while you are there

This example has many back-end sales opportunities. The $25 seminar is the beginning. The $25 sale has identified you as a target for other associated products and services.

It was a means to get you onto the mailing list and as you paid for the privilege, you don't mind getting the mailings, do you? And one day you might even do the three-day course, mightn't you?

Consider how much the sale was worth if you attend the $25 workshop, buy the books, videos and then attend the $1,500 seminar. Were the advertising, coffee, cakes and free pens at the workshop worth the investment? You bet!

Examine the back-end possibilities for your business
Grab a piece of paper and divide it into two columns.

Write down a list of the items you sell in the left-hand column. In the right-hand column, write down the item(s) that could be sold as result of the first sale. Now let's plan a strategy to make these extra sales.

You can do this on Page 12 of your workbook (jamesyuille.com/WYLTSWorkbook).

Customer databases

What information have you recorded about your customers, how do you gather and record it, and how will you make use of it?

If we examine each of these individually, your database might look like this:

Customer Information:
- Name
- Address
- Post Code
- Phone number
- Email
- Age
- Gender
- Marital status
- Children
- Preferred payment method
- Item(s) purchased
- Date(s) of purchase

Method of collection:
- From delivery docket
- From general questions and observation

- From response coupons (e.g. "Privileged customer" club)
- From warranty card

Method of recording:
- Entered electronic database by (person) every week
- Sent to an outsource database management firm
- Online the customer themselves, often motivated by a bonus or cash-back offer.

How this information can be used:
- Generate a "thank you" letter, postcard or note *(highly recommended)*
- Regular mailings (post, fax or email)
- Phone calls to remind customers of service requirements
- Invitations to "exclusive" customer events

Remember

Customer <u>retention</u> is as vital as customer <u>generation</u>.

The effect of reducing customer drop-off by 10% is the same as increasing the number of new customers by 10% *and* it's much cheaper!

Most customers go elsewhere due to perceived indifference. Show them you care and appreciate your custom.

Chapter 13

How to Avoid Being the Next Marketing Victim

Now that you're getting the hang of selling, the next focal point is to ensure that you are getting enough people to talk to. It's important that you have a process (or processes) for generating qualified leads. You need to be meeting and talking with people who are interested in what you have to offer.

Have you ever heard the expression, "50% of the money we spend on marketing is wasted, but we don't know which 50%"? Sometimes this figure is quoted as up to 90%.

Someone who didn't understand testing and measuring said that.

Another fallacy people believe is that if they build a better mousetrap, the world will beat a path to their door. Kevin Costner's famous line, "If you build it, they will come" from the movie, "Field of Dreams" is equally fallacious.

There are hundreds of patented mousetraps but there's still only one kind readily available, the same type we've all been using for years. The point is that unless you have a way to *sell* the better mousetrap, your patent only prevents someone else from copying your mousetrap.

These three statements are among marketing's biggest fallacies.

There are several other great lies told about marketing. Let's look at a few

- That you advertise to create an image
- That you must have a bright, identifiable, colourful logo
- That long copy doesn't sell
- That you shouldn't put an offer in your ad
- That people only buy on price
- That people get tired of your ad
- That you need to keep running an ad because it needs to be seen several times before you get a response

Let's look at these one by one...

Advertising to create an image

One of the many great books I've read is Sergio Zyman's, *The End of Marketing as We Know It*. In case his name's not familiar, Zyman was the Chief Marketing Officer of The Coca-Cola Company. I suppose he knows that most people never finish the books they read, so he makes his most important point in the sub-heading on page 4: Marketing Is Supposed to Sell Stuff.

On the same page he continues with a statement dispelling the idea that advertising is for image. This is Coca-Cola we're talking about, not a small suburban business.

So, if the Chief Marketing Officer of Coca-Cola says that marketing is not about image, it's about sales, that should be good enough for any business owner.

Zyman isn't the only person to say this of course; many have said it before, and others will say it again. What impressed me was that a major league player, not a small business or marketing consultant, made this statement. (We've known this for years because we test and measure.)

Advertising agents tell you that it's about brand and image so they can sell you designs and layouts because that's where they make their money.

They want to keep you coming back for more and different designs. What they don't want is to be held accountable for the results their ads bring you.

Whenever someone tells you marketing is about image or about anything other than making the phone ring or making sales, they're wasting your time and money. Don't walk away, run.

Look for someone who understands that marketing is about sales and getting the phone to ring and talk to them instead.

An accountant friend of mine explains this very clearly when he says, "You can't bank an image; you can only bank cash."

The bright, colourful logo
It helps you get noticed and stand out in the marketplace. It won't help you make sales. When creating adverts, the place to put your logo is in a corner at the bottom of the ad.

The top of the ad should be dominated by your headline which is the advert for the advert. The headline's role is to entice interested readers to read more, and the purpose of the rest of the advert is to encourage the reader to take your preferred course of action – visit your store, call you, complete a form on your website or whatever is your preferred way for them to contact you.

Maybe the ten words you could have put in the same space would have increased your conversion rate by another 0.5% to 1%. I know which I'd rather have.

I'll have every graphic artist in town at my throat for this comment but let me tell you straight: 99% of graphic artists can't write copy. Use a graphic artist for what they do best; graphics. Use a copywriter, or teach yourself to write, for sales copy.

{Sidebar: "Copy" is the phrase used to describe persuasive writing. It differs from "content" which is information writing.}

Get into the habit of writing your copy before you write your headline. Then get the graphic designer to present it.

That long copy doesn't sell
OK, so short copy can sell too, but let's make two key points here...

Long copy does sell but boring, long copy doesn't. It needs to retain the reader's interest.

Because advertising is simply salesmanship in print, let me ask you if you would restrict your best salesperson to the equivalent of a one-page letter to deliver your message verbally?

You wouldn't, would you; you would want as much time as it took.

Long copy does sell and if it didn't, globally successful marketers and copywriters such as Jay Abraham, Dan Kennedy and the late Gary Halbert wouldn't use and advocate it and neither would I.

We keep on doing it because it works. There's no such thing as too-long copy; but there is boring and irrelevant copy. Be clear about the difference.

Write as much copy as it takes, and no more. If you can't write good copy, engage someone who can and be willing to pay them well.

That you don't need an offer in your ad
Unless you give them a reason to call or visit why should they?

During a swarm of ads and competing offers screaming at her to buy, if you haven't given her a reason to act, she won't.

Ads need a call to action. That is; a deadline, a bonus, an extra widget for paying in full – something that gets the reader to act today. Tomorrow it's in the recycling bin and it's too late.

That price is the only issue
I love this one.

Please understand that price is only an issue when there's nothing else to talk about. If price were the only issue, Bugatti, Versace, Gucci and Manolo Blahnik and other prestige brands would all be out of business!

Look at your own purchases; I'll wager YOU don't buy everything on price.

Price is relative, yes, but it's not all. Have this discussion with your clients very early on in your relationship because it's an important issue.

Know the points of difference in the marketplace and make your offers accordingly to remove the need for price comparison.

They (or you) get tired of your ad
They do if they've bought and that doesn't matter because they're no longer in the market. Some ads run unchanged for years.

Here's another key: If your advert keeps on pulling leads, stick with it.

Assess alternatives, and make sure one successful ad is kept as the benchmark. AdWords is a great place to test headlines. It allows you to create more than one advert and to rotate them evenly over a set period to see which gets the best response.

What if *you* get sick of it? You should never get tired of an ad that makes you money!

The ad needs to be run continuously before you get a response

If it doesn't work the first time, it won't work the second. A dud ad is a dud ad.

One of the great, but sad, truths about advertising and copywriting is that not every ad works. Many marketers have faced anguish over the result of what they thought was a "killer" ad or sales letter that flopped.

Nevertheless, there are some strategies you can take to minimise the risk of your copy not working.

Again, using Google Ads, you can inexpensively split-test and research both ads and sales copy. Often as little as $200 in clicks will determine which ad works best. It's far better to test this way then design and print 10,000 brochures only to find they don't work.

Learn to write your own ads and sales letters.

It constantly amazes me when clients say that they let the media rep from the magazine, newspaper or phone directory write their adverts for them. Yes, people still use these media yet somehow don't pay attention to the return on investment. For you to justify the ongoing expense of these media, you must know the numbers.

Similarly, don't let your web developer write the copy and content for your website.

It seems people will spend upwards of $5,000 to buy the media space or to build a great website yet they shy away from investing in good copy to make the advert work – after all, it's just a few words isn't it?

Many businesses don't make the investment in hiring a good copywriter because they fail to understand the value excellent copy brings to their business. Do your research, ask what results they have had for other clients and see samples of their work.

Remember it takes research and time to write quality copy. A copywriter needs to research your product, your market and your competitor before creating the ad or letter.

It wouldn't be unusual for a good copywriter to command a fee of several thousand dollars for a sweet ad or letter. If it gets the result, it's money well spent because you can run the advert or letter again and again and it will continue to generate results.

You wouldn't argue with your lawyer about his fee or the way he wrote that letter for you; you're paying for his knowledge and experience. It's the same with copywriters, don't expect to pay peanuts and get brilliant results; it simply doesn't happen.

When your copywriter submits work for review, only edit it if the facts are wrong. Don't be influenced by a friend or family member who tells you it wouldn't sell them. Their opinion is only valid if they are in the market for your services.

I had a client reject a letter I wrote because his girlfriend didn't like it. He went very silent when I asked him if she was the owner of commercial premises looking for a back-to-base alarm system.

Nobody knows your product or service better than you do. You understand the subtleties and nuances of the marketplace too. By studying copywriting, yourself, expect three key results:

1. You won't get conned by any advertising space salesperson who tries to get you to print a standard name and logo advert.

4. You'll avoid placing adverts in places your customers aren't looking.

5. You might just find the goose that lays the golden egg by following a successful formula and continually testing and measuring.

Study headlines as well; remember that the headline is the most important aspect of the advert or letter. The headline is the advert for the advert. A good headline will stimulate the reader to read on; a poor headline will be ignored.

You understand what your client is buying. You know the emotional appeals. Writing about them in your marketing pieces gives you a far better chance of generating an enquiry than if you stick with the "conventional" adverts most media salespeople and publications want you to use.

My wife fell victim to this some years ago. Having engaged a copywriter and designer to create an advert that was working in a publication, a new editor refused to run the ad again because it didn't fit her new style for the publication.

To her regret, Debra let the editor change her advert to fit their new style. The space cost her over $1,000 and the revised ad did not generate one phone call. If they won't run your advert the way you want it run, cancel the booking.

Even if it takes you a few months to improve your adverts, you're still ahead. Work hard at it; read good materials and you'll dramatically shorten your learning curve.

Take the approach that you're only one great headline away from an avalanche of new business.

Writing direct-mail and advertising campaigns

You are probably thinking that it's time you started to write a direct-mail campaign or create a new advertising campaign. Here are a few steps to follow to get started.

Use a professional to do this for you (or at least buy a book and learn).

If there's one lesson I've learned in my years in sales, it is that writing adverts and direct mail pieces that do the selling for you requires hours of practice. That's why your copywriter's fees are what they are, and why they are worth paying.

Understand that not every letter or ad you write will be a winner! Every week, thousands of dollars are spent in advertising campaigns that don't work. The problem is that their effectiveness isn't measured, and a deluge of money is wasted over and over again.

The important things to remember are:

- Test and measure.
- If a letter or ad doesn't pay for itself, don't use it again.
- It costs the same to run effective instead of ineffective advertising
- All marketing activities are profit centres.

Other considerations include the size of the advert, its placement, the typeface used and the body text. Again, the single most important consideration is the headline. If people don't read your headline; they won't read your copy.

Small, subtle changes to a good headline can increase the response, as you'll see from this simple example.

The simple headline test

Two promotional pieces were sent to the same number of email newsletter subscribers. Which of these two headlines generated the best response?

1. The Secret to Advertising Without Spending Money

 <u>Or</u>
6. Who Else Wants To Advertise Without Spending Money?

One was 32% more effective than the other.

You might have been running the same advert for months, even years and been happy with the result. Yet if this were your advert, for the same investment, your results could have been 32% better.

Those 32% more calls will result in more sales. More sales means more profits. More new clients. More repeat business and more referrals.

Can you pick which headline pulled better?

If you answered number 1, you're right.

"The Secret to Advertising Without Spending Money" generated a 19% response compared with the 13% generated by, "Who Else Wants To Advertise Without Spending Money?"

Shows the importance of headlines, doesn't it? And let me say again, the most important part of the advert or sales letter is the headline.

How did I know which headline worked best? Using my autoresponder I did a "split test" and broadcast half of the articles under one headline and half under the other.

The headline was the only difference between the two emails. One had 8 words, the other 7. On the face of it, they're very similar, yet one outperformed the other by 32%.

As Linda in the TV show "Becker" *(I loved that show!)* would say, *"Here's the thing..."*

How do you know that the headline you're using is the best you could be using?
How many others have you tested?

What would happen if you changed it and scored a 32% increase in enquiries? If your conversion rate were 50%, you would have a 16% increase in sales.

Take this example of a letter used in a law firm. The aim of the letter is to have clients update their Will.

Their headline reads, **"Re: Your Will"**

(Stimulating isn't it?)

Then the letter goes on to talk about the process of updating your Will.

Imagine instead reading this headline: **"What's changed in your life over the last twelve months?"**

This letter goes on to paint pictures of how changing circumstances have an impact on your Will and prompts you to consider what would happen if your life changed and your Will didn't. In other words, it promotes the consequences of not updating your Will. *(Fear of pain.)*

Good copywriters sometimes take days to create a powerful headline for an advert, yet when most business owners write their own headlines, they take seconds or maybe minutes and usually use something inane like the Company name.

They include a photo of what they sell, add details about cost and their phone number and fax it to the newspaper or magazine.

Then wonder why the phone doesn't ring.

Do the same with direct mail too.

A typical in-house, direct-mail piece uses letterhead with an address block and a list of facts about either the company or the product.

It is then posted in an envelope that has a sticky address label on the outside, along with the company's logo and franked postage imprint.

It looks like a direct-mailing piece and will be treated like one, too. Straight into the bin!

Your success in marketing depends on:
1. Attracting readers to your advert.

7. Holding their interest until they reach the end.
8. Having them follow your call-to-action step.

If you're going to use advertising and direct mail to positive effect, then you need a detailed strategy.

Here's a list of some things to consider:
- Who is going to write the copy? (In-house or an external

copywriter?)
- What is the campaign's objective? (What action do you want the client to take; call, walk in, act on a website, register for a webinar)
- Who is the target, and why? (New or existing customers, centres of influence)
- What is the offer? (Discount, extra benefits)
- How to monitor effectiveness? (Financial, numbers, etc.)
- Do all the team, your colleagues, your re-sellers and your suppliers know about the campaign and/or the offer?
- How much are you prepared to spend on it?
- What is the break-even point?
- For how long will it run?
- How easily can it be changed it if it isn't working?
- What are the consequences of it being highly successful?
- How will responses be handled?
- Is there enough stock to fulfil the orders, and if not, what is the availability?
- Can we afford to buy the stock?
- How will sales be supported if the item has to be installed and commissioned?
- What process will be used to finance credit customers?
- What other upside/downside risks are involved?
- How does this advert fit into the long-term plan?

Remember a campaign comprises of more than one advert or mailing piece

To have significant impact on your marketplace, budget for multiple activities over a year or more.

Marketing consultants' opinions vary on how long, how much, what frequency etc.

That's why we measure first. Monitor the effectiveness of your campaign. Each activity should be tracked by recording all calls, responses, visits, sales etc., so you can gauge the potential long-term outcomes.

Financial outcomes need to be measured to determine if the same campaign should be used in other markets, in other states or countries, or adapted to suit other products. Remember the adage, "What you can't measure, you can't manage!"

This especially applies to advertising and marketing, areas where you can waste thousands of dollars not analysing the results.

Once you see a trend that shows a certain combination headline, message, offer, guarantee is more successful than others and is making money, use that combination as a benchmark and try to beat it.

Well-resourced marketing is the driving force behind successful companies.

Know your two most critical marketing numbers:
1. **Cost of customer acquisition.** To calculate, divide last year's total marketing expense by the number of new customers gained.

9. **Lifetime value of the customer.** How much that customer spends with you over a five-year period, and how much profit it brings?

There is an exercise to help you with this on Page 1 of your workbook (jamesyuille.com/WYLTSWorkbook).

When you know the cost of client acquisition, you know how to measure the effectiveness of any marketing activity. You can create a control price figure to match and try to beat.

When you know a client's lifetime value, you know the return on your acquisition investment.

You will fail fast if you spend more on gaining the customer than their lifetime value brings you.

It is essential to measure the effectiveness of your advertising. It has only one purpose – to generate revenue. Advertising for image is a total waste of money.

Use coupons or codes; ask people to cut vouchers out, train the person who answers the phone to ask from which ad they're calling.

Understand that customers know they have a choice, but they don't know how to decide. As a result, they decide on price. It's your job to help them decide, based on other factors, and when you do, price is no longer the issue.

The importance of creating, maintaining, and managing a customer database cannot be emphasised enough. Far too few retailers, restauranteurs and service companies do this. As a result, they're always chasing new business instead of retaining the customers they've already got.

Once you have a customer database, however big or small, use it to stay in touch with them. How often? It depends upon your business but monthly is easy. Of course, specials can be used out of sequence.

Use a combination of phone calls, postcards, email (via your Autoresponder), letters and direct sales letters. Put some YouTube videos featuring testimonials from satisfied clients on your website. Promote a webinar.

Remember the upsell. McDonald's are famous for their upsell line: "Did you want fries with that?" What's your upsell line? *(We covered that earlier – remember the examples of the measuring cup and the toothbrush / toothpaste?)*

Internet marketing myths exploded

There's probably more mystique about this than any other marketing tool in history. Fewer and fewer people say they don't trust the internet and won't buy online. Millions of people are using it every day to find businesses like yours. As I write this manuscript, the latest figures are that worldwide, Google process over 40,000 enquiries *per second*.

If you aren't there when they search, your competitors will be.

Again, if you're not actively present on the internet, you're running a very serious risk. Today's buyers seek information before making purchase decisions. Customers will come to you armed with more knowledge than at any time in history and won't take you seriously if you're trying to use antiquated sales techniques with them.

A new car my wife bought was thoroughly researched on the Internet before she even visited a showroom to decide from which dealer to purchase it. She knew how much the car was, what her trade-in was worth and knew how to drive the deal. She recently bought a washing machine the same way.

My sons buy almost everything online. If there wasn't a Coles supermarket 100 metres from their inner Melbourne apartment, they would probably buy groceries online too. The only reason they go to a shop is because they need it today. If it's not needed today, they buy online because even from the other side of the world, delivery is so efficient.

The internet is another marketing tool. It can work brilliantly for you when you make these four simple decisions:

1. Decide what your site must do for you

Is it to inform, to sell, to entertain, to promote?

2. Decide who you want to have as visitors

This is your customer demographic. Colours, language, patterns, and layout may need to be specific for certain markets.

3. Work out how people will find it

You can promote websites in a wide variety of ways but the most important are Organic (or Natural) search, where the Search Engines find your site and list you in the top few sites in your category, and Pay-Per-Click promotion where you pay every time someone clicks on your search engine advertising links.

Recent changes to Google's search results page, together with the increasing use of Google Business listings (previously Places) and aggregator sites mean organic listings are becoming harder to achieve.

4. Decide what you want visitors to do when they get there

Do you want them to purchase something immediately or would you prefer them to call you or complete a form?

Let's also dispel several other myths about websites...

- Design is all-important
- They don't need many words if they look good
- They should be full of links
- They're hard to build
- They need an entry page
- You shouldn't try to sell anything from your site; it's there for information

- They cost thousands of dollars and even then, are a bottomless pit of expense
- Functionality is irrelevant

Design is all-important

Yes, it counts but not before content. Search engines don't look for design. They look for content. It's far better to have a plain site with highly relevant content than a well-designed site with no content. It's also 100% vital that the site be fully mobile-responsive.

It's like the myths of advertising and copywriting; design is great for designers. Content and compelling copy count for marketing results.

If you're hiring or have hired a Web Designer, be aware that you've got a Designer on your hands, not necessarily a Web Developer or a Marketer.

These are all different specialities. Web designers are just that; they design things. Their focus is on appearance, not performance. Developers create code and custom functionalities. Markers understand how to get the visitor to act.

Find a developer who understands marketing.

Leaving the construction of your website to a family friend or relative just because they know a bit about IT is not good enough. As with copywriting, find a professional and pay them well.

Sites don't need many words providing they look good

If you can make the same number of sales with half the words, remove half the words. If that works, try taking all the words away and see how many sales your great design and wonderful graphics make you.

Hmmm, thought so...

You need as many words as it takes to get the response you want. No less.

They should be full of links
So your visitors can escape and surf someone else's site? That's OK if they are Affiliate Links that make you money otherwise, you're waving potential customers goodbye. Once they leave your site they aren't coming back.

They need a special entry page
Reality check here: while you're entertaining your potential clients with a page of moving graphics that navigates the magic, "Enter Here" button around the page, most of your potential visitors have gone.

They've come for information, not entertainment.

Give them easy access to the information.

You shouldn't try to sell from your site
What else is it for? Your site's key task, surely, is to gain their attention long enough to have them buy or at least generate an enquiry. **Why then have it?**

If you're insistent on building a business website for any other purpose than to help make sales, support your team or generate enquiries, *save the money and go on a fishing trip instead.*

It costs thousands of dollars to build a site
Unless you need a large e-Commerce platform, or something equally as sophisticated, a professionally built commercial website should set you back $3,000 to $5,000.

You should make sure that whomever you choose to build your site has a clear understanding of you, your product and your target market.

You should also ask if the content management system they use will allow you to make swift changes to your copy, or to add pages quickly if a market opportunity presents itself.

Check their turn-around time for adding content if you want them to do it for you. Sometimes, even two days delay in posting new copy to your site can cause you to miss the boat.

An example would be a glazier wanting to add a page relating to hailstorm damage response. He'd want to put an ad on Google and to direct the clicks to an appropriate landing page. He'd want to do that literally overnight as hundreds of potential customers will be looking for him.

Beware of some do-it-yourself content management systems. As with copywriting, you all too frequently get what you pay for. Some proprietary content management systems don't allow you access to things like, Meta tags and page description codes. Both are essential to getting good search engine listings. Unless you have a special reason not to, stick with common content management systems like Joomla or WordPress.

Many providers and DIY solutions don't allow you to easily add many new technologies such as audio and video or subscription boxes. Their solutions either haven't kept up with the times, or they don't understand the marketing process. Sometimes it's both....

Compare the up-front cost of a well built, automated website with the annual phone directory or with display advertising in a colourful magazine or trade journal. Your website works for you

24/7 and never phones in sick. What's more, once it's built, all you need to do is keep it up to date.

That it's an ongoing money drain.
Only if you do it wrong from the beginning. It's just another marketing tool; get it right and it will keep on working for you. You may have to fiddle a bit but by making sure you have a system you can change yourself, it's an easy task to delegate.

Used effectively, the internet can drive prospects to you by the busload, far cheaper than you can gather them any other way. What's more, they are qualified prospects because they've taken time to search for you, read your offer and then make contact. Why, they're almost totally pre-sold!

Just recently, using pay-per-click advertising on Google, in one week we drove 324 prospects to an industrial product site at just 39 cents each. Prospects don't come much cheaper than 39 cents each...

You will of course, have the ongoing costs of hosting. You may also choose to pay by the month for other services such as your autoresponder, payment gateway or shopping cart. Even were it to cost you as much as $100 per month, if it's delivering you high quality leads, that's still cheap.

That websites are hard to build
They're not. They can be time-consuming however, and you need to do your research before you start. What research?

You must find know what your potential clients are searching for. The bad news is that getting a direct hit is unlikely unless you've already communicated with them by means of an ad, mailing piece, business card etc. so you need to spend some time doing keyword research.

Spend time using Google's keyword research tool available when you create an account at ads.google.com

These tools help you identify what terms your potential visitors are searching for. By matching the key words and phrases, the page titles and the headlines to their search, you'll be easier to find and more relevant to your buyers.

If you're going to get someone else to build your site, make sure they do it to your specifications, not theirs. Do your homework first, not later.

Remember

Whatever you do, wherever you plan to publish your message, first consider this question:

"What is your Most Desired Response?"

In other words, "What do you want visitors to do when they read your sales message?"

Chapter 14

How to Use The Power of Others to Your Advantage

Develop a pipeline of people who have a natural need for your services, or who can help you find these people in other ways. When people refer you to their friends, associates and family, it puts you and the new prospect on common ground immediately.

Learn to look for them in unconventional ways. Virtually every contact you meet can provide you with a referral or useful information of some sort if you ask the right questions.

A word of caution: if someone along the way asks you what you are selling, always tell them the truth. "I'm selling Insurance." When they reply, "I already have Insurance" it tells you that they believe in what you sell!

How can you generate referrals?

The best time to ask for referrals is when you've just done business with someone. But you can ask at other times too.

After each sale, simply turn to a blank page in your diary or notebook and say, "Just like you, my business depends on meeting people. Would you please give me the names of two others who, like you, would be interested in (detail the consequence gained)?"

Sit and wait quietly with an expectant, confident smile. You will get them. Maybe not two, and maybe not every time, but you will get them.

A friend of mine starts the conversation with a referral request. Outrageous you might say. Yes, but it works for him. Here's what he says: "Before we start, I'm going to ask you a favour. If we agree to do business, I'm going to ask you to give me the names of ten people who would benefit from this service. Is that OK with you?" Believe it or not, it works. Test it. What have you to lose?

Once you have gathered all these referrals, make sure you call them.

Use your business cards liberally. Give them away in twos, one for the person you just met and one for them to give away.

Try writing, "thank you" on the card too. When you are asked why, just smile and reply, "It's to say thanks for the opportunity to assist you."

If you don't ask for referrals, you won't get any!

Why referral business is so valuable

1. Customers who refer are more likely to stay with you and as a result, spend more, adding to their lifetime value.
2. Referrals are more likely to become customers. Why? Because they have been recommended to you by someone they trust and who in turn, trusts you.
3. Referrals who become clients are likely in turn to generate referrals because they understand the process and appreciate that someone cared enough to refer them to you.

The best way to generate referrals is to earn them! You have to treat your customers as friends. The result is that they will want to introduce you to people they know who in turn can do business with you.

It's back to that Trust thing again isn't it? Remember the equation, R=M (Relationships equal Money). By showing you care about them and about their lives, your level of trust increases. Before doing business with you, people will ask themselves these questions about you and your business:

1. Do I like them?
2. Do I respect them?
3. Can I trust them?

Maybe not consciously, but the reason they do, or don't do, business with you is in the answers to these questions.

By taking the time to develop relationships, trust increases, as does the likelihood of referrals.

When delivering a high standard of service in an appropriate professional environment or fashion, you are demonstrating your professional competence. The combination of this and your capacity to develop relationships will in turn earn you the right to ask for referrals.

I guarantee that if you began asking your customers for referrals on a regular basis you would instantly see an increase in referrals coming into your business.

Another suitable time to ask for a referral is when a customer gives you a compliment or expresses any kind of gratitude towards you or your business.

If you're not confident, just ask anyway as the more times you do something, the better you get at doing it. It will help your business.

Tell them that your purpose in asking is to build your business. There is absolutely nothing wrong with that and clients who really like you will feel honoured that you have asked for their help.

Be confident in telling your clients who they should be thinking of as referrals (e.g. people under a lot of stress, people who are health-conscious, people in pain), and be specific. You get what you ask for!

OK, so now you've gained enough trust and respect to ask for referrals, what do you do when you start getting them?

Simple. Make a fuss of them by means of reward and recognition. Just as with children and dogs, rewarding good behaviour makes certain that the behaviour is repeated! Gift baskets, restaurant vouchers or movie vouchers make suitable referral rewards, however, keep in mind the need to be commensurate with the amount of the sale. A word of caution; be careful if someone asks for payment for providing referrals. It could be construed later as a hidden commission with negative consequences and with potential tax implications.

Do it publicly, too. Create a Referral Recognition wall in your reception area. Put the names of people you've rewarded up there. Run a referral incentive program that rewards more, for more referrals.

Remember we're talking about the cost of client acquisition and retention here. Far better to pay for the client after they've spent than to gamble on attracting them!

Testimonials
When they are genuine, testimonials are powerful tools. Testimonials are "raving fans" talking about you and what you do to everyone including those who haven't heard of you or used your product/service before.

Testimonials should be requested from customers who have told you how pleased they are with what you have done for them.

This is the first written testimonial I ever received for sales training:

> " It is now over nine months since I received training in sales and business development from you. The techniques you taught and the 'consultative selling' philosophy you imparted have continued to provide results.
>
> Upon your advice I made small and simple changes to my sales process. The result was immediate, and I very shortly made my first sale. I then made six more sales in rapid succession. Since then I have continued to apply your techniques and record steady and consistent sales.
>
> Thank you for your assistance."
>
> David Newington, Docwise Information Management, Brisbane.

David had a great software product that just wasn't selling.

Why?

He was selling the sausage instead of the sizzle. He wasn't taking time to establish the problem and instead was peddling a product instead of a solution.

With a little help from me, and with understanding of TIPS and the Theory of Consequence, David took Docwise forward at a rapid rate.

David has long since sold Docwise. He went into the travel industry with Flight Centres where he rose rapidly to the position of Corporate Sales Manager and managed the most successful corporate sales team in Australia before relocating to America and working with FCM Travel.

The last I heard of David he was CEO of Flight Centre's Asian operations in Singapore.

When using testimonials, the inclusion of the author's full name rather than their initials adds credibility. *David Newington* is far more credible than *D.N. of Brisbane*.

Adding the company name, logo, and location, or in the case of a residential referral, their suburb, again increases their credibility.

Many websites today include photos of testimonial referees as well as videos of their product endorsement.

You may find that asking your customers to write a testimonial for you proves to be a challenge for them. They may say they don't know what to write. That's OK; simply ask them to jot down a few words about the positive experience of buying from you.

You can even go to the extent of asking them to explain it to you verbally. Then just transfer their statement into a Word file and have them print it onto their letterhead and sign it if they're happy to.

The key to a successful testimonial comes from this formula: "Once I was lost, now I am found"

By explaining the problem, they were experiencing before you came along, and how you solved it for them, your testimonials will enable you to identify with more people.

Centres of influence

Who do you know (or can you get to know) who could be a centre of influence for you? Someone who knows the kind of people you would like to meet and sell to. Those that have a need for what you sell.

Develop your confidence to the point where you can even ask relative strangers for information. Ask someone you've just met, "I want to visit some other people in this area about my product. If you were me, who would you call on next?"

Let's look at some possibilities. These spheres of influence include some surprises. Think about who each of these people within your community knows...

- Mechanics know people who owns cars
- Real Estate people know who has just moved in or out of the area
- Accountants know about business owners
- Photographers know people who have recently married or had children
- Caterers know who is holding functions
- HR and outplacement consultants know who is hiring and firing
- Florists know people who are celebrating

Ask open questions.

Start with, "Who do you know who... "
Here are some examples. Who do you know who...?
- Is getting married?
- Is buying a new house?
- Is buying a new truck?
- Is about to have their first child?

Write down a list of ten, "Who do you know..." you could ask that would gain you useful, relevant information. Formulate the questions so that they ask about people of the same profile as people who buy your service.

Always write down any names they give you and remember to ask for details of how to contact them. Obtain addresses, phone numbers, and places of business or employment. Note any contact details that will assist you to access them.

Social media platforms make this much easier than it has ever been. Using LinkedIn for example, you can ask your contacts to put you in touch with people they know who fit your customer profile. Do your research first and establish to whom you would like an introduction. Most times your contacts will be happy to oblige.

To help generate referrals, people must be able to easily describe who you are and what you do. They must easily understand the "idea" of your company. If people quickly grasp the idea and benefits of your business, it's considered to be infectious.

How smooth is your company's pitch? Do people nod knowingly as you describe your company's products or services, or do they look puzzled and quickly excuse themselves?

Here are some pointers to help you identify how your client sees your product/services...

- Interview (or have a third-party interview) your current satisfied customers.
- Ask customers to describe the situation (and pain), which first motivated them to buy your product/service.
- Ask customers to describe the value of your products or services.
- Ask customers how they describe your business to others.

- Write down exactly, word-for-word, the answers to these questions.
- Reframe your infomercials using the pain points and description of how customers describe your services to others.
- Test and refine your pitch whenever you meet someone new.
- Use your refined pitch in your marketing materials.

Marketing is the driving force of any company. It is the only function that generates revenue – cash! Every other function is an expense that costs you money.

Remember

Engrave this question into your permanent memory:

"Who else knows my prospect?"

(Let me just add one more comment here…those five words, "Who else knows my customer?" are like liquid gold. It's not just who you know, it's who they know that matters…)

Chapter 15

How To Impress Anyone Inside 60 Seconds

You may belong to a business referral group such as BNI, Leads Club, Chamber of Commerce, Rotary etc. At these meetings, whether as a member or as a guest, you often have the opportunity to introduce yourself and what you do. At the very least you will meet people before or after these functions so be prepared and know what to say.

Generally, you'll either get 30 or 60 seconds to do this and so the plan is to maximise the effectiveness of that speaking time. At some groups, you will have the opportunity to ask for a referral too.

Sometimes this is part of the same introductory speech; sometimes it's a different speech. Either way, you need to be prepared because the first impression you give is the most important.

The Infomercial or Elevator Speech - What is it and what's in it for me?

It's an opportunity for you to promote who you are and what you do to an interested audience. Done well, it's a huge revenue source for you.

What should it contain?

If your infomercial is to contain a referral request, it should include these elements. Delete or rearrange them to suit your group's protocols.

1. Who you are, what you do and the Company you own or represent?

4. Describe the services you provide
5. Outline your ideal client
6. Outline a special or seasonal event (optional)
7. Describe who you'd like to meet (your referral)
8. Close and add your USP

Make the key statement the most powerful you can about your product or service.

Promote the WIIFM (What's In It For Me?) aspect of your business.

Assume you have the challenge to tell me in 30 seconds; what makes you different; how do you stand out?

I'm doing one here using a bookkeeping business as an example. Substitute your own details of course…

Step 1: Your introduction

Start with your name and state that you represent Speedy Bookkeeping.

"Good morning/afternoon/hello, I'm Suzie Jackson, of XYZ Commercial Realty."

(I suggest you don't say, "My name is…" Using, "I'm Suzie Jackson… " is more powerful.) Better still, "Suzie Jackson…" is even more powerful!

Step 2: Describe your service

Next add something about your service or product. Make a definitive statement – remember if it's true and you say it first, you own it!

You should explain where you work and that you visit clients at their place of business. Here's an example...

"I work throughout the Valley area and visit clients at their business premises by appointment five days a week between 7am and 6pm."

Now describe the services you provide. Don't cover too many different ones – just one at a time (e.g. selling commercial property, leasing commercial property, acting as a buyer's agent for commercial property purchases) Try to express what you do in terms of customer benefits, like this...

"When you need to find a new warehouse, let me act for you and conduct the lease negotiation so you get the best terms possible."

Step 3: Outline your ideal client

Tell the group who your ideal client is. Think about this one because what you ask for, you invariably get!

"My ideal client is a local owner-operated business employing ten to fifteen staff"

Step 4: Outline a special or seasonal event

If appropriate, document some, "special events" messages to add when in season.

"With the upcoming legislative changes to commercial property lease conditions, let me review your lease to see what impacts there may be."

Step 5: Describe your ideal referral for this week

If you've outlined a seasonal or special event you MUST seek a related referral.

"Typically, an independent retailer appreciates this kind of assistance and your referral to retailers would be appreciated."

There are two kinds of referrals, direct and indirect. A direct referral is where you get introduced to someone with whom you can do business.

An indirect referral is one where you are introduced to someone who knows people with whom you can do business. Be aware that you should identify both in your rotational referral requests and frequently, indirect referrals can be better in the long-term than direct referrals.

Step 6: Closing off

"Suzie Jackson, of XYZ Commercial Realty, the Valley district's leading commercial realty specialist. Make sure you always have my card with you."

Now finish with your USP (Unique selling proposition) or your "memory hook" which is a simple, catchy slogan by which people can remember you.

When you find one that gets a positive reaction from the group, stick to it.

Summary
- Your intro and close should remain unchanged.
- Rehearse this every week until it's both within time and automatic and you've got the perfect 60 - second infomercial!
- Your homework task is to create several along the same

lines…

Next time someone asks you who you are and what you do, it's ready.

You can craft your own on Page 14 of your workbook (jamesyuille.com/WYLTSWorkbook).

Some generic dos and don'ts

- Don't overwhelm people with your initial enthusiasm when you first join the group. Rather, take a few weeks to watch and learn.
- Individually, invite members for a coffee with the idea of finding out about their businesses. Whatever you do, don't try to sell your services to them on this occasion (unless they specifically ask you to do so).
- When seeking referrals, never say you want to meet "someone" or "anyone". These people don't exist. Instead, be specific. Indeed, the more specific, the better. For example, if you want to meet the local bank manager, say so. Chances are that someone will know just the person you want to meet.
- Work hard at eliminating these words from your presentation – I, Me, We, Our. Instead, phrase your sentences in, "you" terms. Count the number of times you use I, Me, We, Our, as opposed to You and Your. You and Your should significantly exceed I, Me, We, and Our.
- Within your referral group, your service will have different appeals to different people. Try to think how best your services will advantage each member. As an example, a finance or mortgage broker will appreciate your ability to produce financial statements to support loan applications.

Your 10-minute presentation

At some stage, you may be asked to deliver a 10-minute presentation about yourself and your services. A good idea is to include a series of questions members can use to identify potential clients for you. Here are a couple of examples:

- "Do you find negotiating property leases for your business frustrating?"
- "What is the single biggest frustration you have as a commercial property landlord?"

Make your talk both interesting and informative. Try to tell them something they don't know. You might create a quiz to show members that mistakes in lease documents are easily made and it takes an expert to find and eliminate them.

With a brilliant infomercial you can:

- Explain what you do in 60 seconds or less
- Differentiate yourself from the competition
- Generate referral business easily and quickly
- Make a great first impression

Remember

You NEVER get a second chance to make a first impression.

Take time to make sure your first impression is memorable – for the right reasons!

Chapter 16

How to Deliver Awesome Customer Service

Over the last 30 years, I've worked in, managed, and owned several different businesses. My focus has always been on sales and one concept I've instilled into everyone with whom I've worked is that the task of gaining and retaining customers is not just the salesperson's mission: it's **everyone's**!

The nature of the business doesn't matter.

You can be running an accountancy practice, law firm or a natural health care clinic; be involved in computer maintenance, dog washing or hair care; operating a café, fitness centre or a consultancy as I do. It doesn't matter. The fundamentals are the same.

Non-sales staff get confused because they see the function of their job, be it maintenance technician or accounts clerk, as unrelated to the revenue generation aspect of the business.

Nothing could be further from the truth.

This is a very important concept; one that few businesses really grasp and yet it's a major cause of the breakdown in the process of creating and maintaining long-term client relationships.

My purpose is to explain by use of real-life examples, how easily the supplier/client relationship can be enhanced or destroyed.

In his book, *Critical Path,* R. Buckminster Fuller outlined a formula for working out the number of relationships within a group of people. Bearing in mind that x represents the number of people, here's the formula:

Number of relationships = x^2 minus x

Suppose you have four staff and they're all involved with six staff members from a client company. There are a total of 90 relationships involved. Hard to imagine? Yes, and that's why everyone involved in your business needs to fully understand this concept.

Let's start by making a couple of general statements about running a business.

Any business owner knows that the aim of the business is to generate profit, preferably lots of it.

Before that can happen though, the business must have an income.

- Revenue comes from making sales.
- Sales come from customers.
- Repeat sales are made to satisfied customers.
- Profits come when overheads and costs are less than sales revenue.

It stands to reason therefore, that to make profits, the business needs to find and keep customers.

To continue to make profits, and for profits to increase, you can either reduce overheads or make more sales.

The truth about reducing overheads is that you can only go so far – you can cut the phone and power bills and possibly reduce other expenses but that may only reduce costs by 5%, making little difference to the profit line - so all you can really do is sell more or buy better. Buying better isn't all that easy, so the solution is to make more sales.

Any business without customers won't be able to put a single dollar in your pocket. It won't matter if you have an honours degree or the best product on the planet.

No customers = no cash flow

For the sake of simplicity, I want to focus on the *customer* aspect. After all, without the customer we'd have no revenue and therefore no business.

Some business planning purists would say that the starting point of the enterprise is a vision, a goal of where we want to be in two, five, ten years. That's fine, but in the everyday battle of making money, those admirable aspirations are forgotten; especially by the staff whose main motivation is their next pay.

In real terms, we're dealing with the day-to-day interaction between your staff and your revenue source. Remember that most of your staff members don't share your vision or aspirations. When you look at it like that, what they do and say suddenly becomes important, doesn't it?

Yet typically we don't take any time to train our support teams in customer communication skills.

Here's a great way to alienate callers:

"Please can I speak with Mrs xxx?"

"Do you have a name?" comes the reply.

"Yes I have." *(Of course I have...)*

Why not simply ask, "Please can I let him/her know who is calling?" or, "May I ask who is calling so I can introduce you?"

I'd give them my name. I'd then expect that when I'm connected, the recipient would know my name. Why doesn't that always happen? Don't you hate it when asked your name and then you find that you've not been introduced?

Simple mistakes but they all infuriate your callers who are your revenue stream, your profit source. Likewise, clients hate it when they leave a message and you don't call back.

If I'm looking to spend money with you. The least you can do is call me back. When everyone has a mobile phone, a voicemail service, SMS facilities and email, not returning calls is inexcusable.

Here's a test for you: **get a friend to call your office when you're not there.**

Ask them what happens. You'll likely be surprised. That's the purpose of a mystery shopper. To tell you what you probably didn't want to hear!

I made a call to a Company recently because of seeing their advert and asked about their products.

A male voice very enthusiastically answered all my questions and also told me who their competitor was when he said, "We're cheaper than Company X too". He didn't even bother to get my name. You can guess the name of the Company I called next...

Another male voice answered my call at Company X. He asked who I was and what my interest in their product was.

I told him and he asked me a few more questions before recommending a solution. He then asked if I had internet access and directed me through their website to let me see more about it.

Then he walked me through the site with the result being, I did business. It's obvious why, isn't it?

Let's start with some examples of good service...

This one demonstrates an understanding of the lifetime value of a customer. Put simply, lifetime value relates to the total spend that client can make with you over the years you'll do business together.

When my focus was solely on sales training, I had a client who had been with me for over five years. The first sale was only about $5,000 but over time, their total spend has been well more than $45,000 and they have generated at least five other substantial clients for me through referrals.

That's a valuable client.

Here's another:

A lawnmower man was driving down my street one Sunday and saw me pruning some bushes in the yard with a handsaw. He stopped, grabbed his chain saw and started to help. I asked him how much he wanted, and he said, *"Nothing mate. I was on my way to the tip and the trailer isn't full"*.

He knows the value of a customer. Gary has cut my lawn on average 20 times a year for about ten years. I paid him $25 per mow - that's over $5,000 so I guess a free load to the tip wasn't that much to give away. He saved me having to borrow or hire a trailer and from spending my afternoon going to the tip.

A couple of pages further on I'll reveal how I show owners of businesses like this to build their customer base quickly and effortlessly.

And another…

I had a flat tyre. More than flat, it was destroyed because I reversed into the sharp edge of a storm water drain.

Anyway, in trying to change the tyre, I couldn't undo the wheel nuts. I had to call a tow truck! We took the car to Bob Jane T-Mart where I had bought the tyres. They removed the nuts, reporting that they were fastened on too tightly.

It occurred to me that they had been the last to remove the wheels and I started to discuss the inconvenience with the store manager. He explained how with their specialist equipment this problem couldn't occur and he asked me if anyone else might have taken the wheels off.

It was then I realised that the car dealer had done a brake replacement a few weeks before and the problem was likely to have been caused then.

I paid for the tyre and drove off to see the dealer, explaining the situation. They checked wheel nuts and found them all far too tight. Accepting that the inconvenience had been due to their initial error, they refunded the cost of the tyre.

Why? Because apart from anything else, the episode had made them aware of an internal problem. Checking other vehicles serviced at around the same time showed that some had suffered from the same problem. (The report on the Bob Jane invoice certainly helped.)

Bob Jane T-Mart knew how to do it right. As it is to McDonald's, to Bob Jane T-Marts, customer service is everything. If you ever wonder why companies like these get to be so big and so successful, that's how. Their systems are entrenched, bullet-proof and reliable. Their employees are trained and understand that everyone has a role in customer generation and retention. There's a message in that.

Therein lies a simple theme: both these companies understand the lifetime value of their customer. Each experience has to be good to make sure you return.

Here's an example of what should happen to build revenue and customer loyalty in a café.

When you see two or more people earnestly engaged in a conversation long after their coffee is finished, move to the table to collect the dirty cups and unobtrusively say, "You look like you're here for a while. Shall I get you another?"

A sceptical client agreed to try this and the first time he did, he **almost doubled** the day's takings. He added an extra twist because when taking the second cup back, he presented a small selection of cakes on a tray and said, "Can I tempt you?"

Simple, effective, and profitable, and it creates goodwill with customers. They come back because you've looked after them.

Here's how you can quickly create a profitable lawn mowing, window cleaning or other direct-to-customer service business.

1. Identify a suitable customer in a nearby street to where you live.

9. Offer the first couple of services free.
10. Visit every other nearby house with the potential to buy.

11. Explain that you're doing number 46 and that if they get theirs done next time you're in the street, they'll get 10% off.
12. Continue with nearby homes or offices until you have a full day's work.
13. Repeat again in other nearby streets until fully booked. Now you're busy every day with little or no travelling.

Think it won't work?

Try. You'll be very surprised.

When my sons were young, Jeff Lee opened a Barber's Shop in Sunnybank Hills. I went for a haircut in the first week his shop was open and took my sons soon after.

The three of us went there once a month over those 10 years, that's a total of 360 haircuts between us. Jeff's prices were reasonable, averaging $12 - $15 each. In a ten-year period, that's over $3,500. A visit to Jeff's was always fun, never without a laugh and he's a great barber too.

Jeff was clever. He realised that Monday mornings were quiet, so he offered an aged pensioner $7 haircut promotion. Word spread and soon you couldn't get near the shop on Mondays. It turned into a meeting place for the "old boys" of the neighbourhood. *(The leggy blonde Jeff had working with him didn't harm the promotion.)*

The local Optometrist/Eyewear Shop, "Eyes Fantastic" was similar. My wife and I both wore glasses and over the same ten-year period we averaged one pair each per year. I guess we spent over $4,000 with them in that time. My oldest son, my sister, my mother, and many of our friends go there. (I no longer wear glasses, cataract surgery fixed that!)

They're good, friendly, trustworthy people who always walk the extra mile to make sure your frames are just right.

I went shopping for a new pair of shoes. Nothing difficult about that you'd think, but in just one big shopping mall I walked out of three stores.

Why?

No one approached despite me taking shoes off the display and trying them on. Amazing! You'd think they didn't want to make the sale!

In the fourth store it was different. I handled a pair of shoes and a young lady called, 'Katie' came over and asked if they were my size. I nodded. Katie offered a shoehorn to help me put them on and then said something surprising.

Picking up the shoe I'd taken off (a black brogue) she said, "Isn't it funny that when you put the old one beside the new pair how tired it looks?"

"Yes" I replied.

"Let me show you how to fix that" she said, reaching over to her counter.

"Watch this." She took the cover off a Colorado shoe wax pad and ran it over my old shoe.
It immediately looked like new.

"Great. Now do the other one for me."

"When you buy the new pair I will," she said with a rakish smile and ran the pad over the brown shoe I had tried on. "See, it even makes that one look better".

"Wrap them up, I'll take them, and you'd better put a couple of those cleaners in, too." Katie smiled, cleaned my other shoe, and wrapped them up. I never asked how much the wax pads were. They were about $12 each, adding a nice sweetener to the sale.

Now some not-so-good customer service...

At 8.30am a wealthy client, due to make a presentation to the local council at nine, walked into a store that sold photocopiers and provided a copy service. He wanted to make a back-up copy of his lengthy presentation.

The shop appeared to be open: doors were unlocked, lights and machines on, etc, but the young lady who met him said she couldn't do photocopies until 9 am because that's when the copy centre opened for business.

What did he do?

He walked down the road to the Library and did them himself at 10 cents per page, spending $11.00.

Guess where he won't look to buy his next copier?

A friend told me that he walked into a bakery/café with a client at 4.50 pm and asked for two take-away coffees and two slices of cake. He was told they could only have the cake to take-away as the shop closed at 5 and coffee took too long to make and drink.

They left and went elsewhere. The irony is that my friend's client is a local council alderman and the Deputy Mayor owns the shop.

The owner of a local café I often visited went on holidays and hung a sign in the window, "Have taken 10 days holiday. We knew you'd understand".

I understood.

I went around the corner, discovered a new café that has given me a voucher for a free coffee for every five I buy. I've been back frequently and have enjoyed several bonus cups!

I did a mortgage transaction and **three representatives failed to follow up.** One was my own bank with which I had my previous loan. The second was a major national loan originator and an accountant friend recommended the third.

The successful vendor was a broker to whom I was referred. He did everything I asked (and more) within the time frame I needed and went out of his way to explain just how the loan worked.

The Bank of Queensland advertised for some time with these two questions:
1. Who's your bank manager?

14. What's their phone number?

The point being made was that they offer a personal service. They're reacting positively to customers who are sick of voice-prompted customer support centers; the ones that have eleven prompts telling you to press 3, 6, 4 or # before spitting out, 'you're third in the queue and the estimated waiting time is eleven minutes.'

Compare how easy it is to open an online account with PayPal in comparison with a, "real world" bank. It took me just a few minutes. Recently wanting a credit card merchant facility with my own bank, it took nine emails, five phone calls and two weeks to get it done.

How easy is it for your clients to do business with you? Do your processes create obstacles and stumbling blocks for people to negotiate or are they simple? Is your business user-friendly.

When they enter a store or your restaurant, do they know how to go about a transaction? I was once about to walk out of a café because no one had come to take my order until finally one of the staff told me I had to go to the counter to place my order!

Why didn't I know that already? Because in the ten minutes I sat there, I was the only customer. Don't you think they could have come to see me earlier?

If you have a store, you would know that the worst thing you can say to a customer is, "Can I help you?" The universal answer is, "No, just looking" isn't it?

Why not turn it around and say this?

"Hi, is this your first time here?" If they reply that it is, you can then take a few seconds to explain how it works and invite them to fill out a coupon or to call you over if they need information. This is non-threatening and results in a positive, lasting impression.

Sadly, there's not a lot of real selling done in today's retail environment. Very few employees behave as proactively as Katie in my shoe-store example.

I found another one recently at a department store when buying shirts and ties with a gift voucher. A lady called, 'Irene' who really knew her stuff, taught me how to spot a well-made tie from a poorly made tie in a couple of minutes.

Sadly though, Irene is an exception in a retail world where apathy abounds. Even in stores where staff members get paid commissions, not much selling is going on. There is certainly no database collection.

Here is another example. My sons are very keen basketball players. Both played in school and club teams and were district representative players.

They trained and played all year round. They chewed through footwear. Both had at least two pairs of basketball shoes, one for training and the second for playing. Invariably we bought them from one of two both national brand retailers.

The Nike shoes they preferred were not cheap, yet in the stores from which we bought, we were never asked our names and consequently never received any promotional offers.

I recall we bought four to six pairs of basketball shoes every year. At $200 or so per pair, that's a lot of money and over ten years, a small fortune.

{Sidebar: Holy smoke: that's over $12,000 in *shoes*! Damn, basketball was expensive!}

How easy would it be for the store to lock us in by offering a loyalty card program or by having a mailing list promoting new shoes at the start of the season?

Some years ago, I gave a sports shoe-store client the idea of presenting all his shoe types together. They were mixed up like Brown's cows. He put the entire range of cross-trainers in one place, all the running shoes in another, etc. Unique then; common practice today.

As a result, when customers started browsing, they were able to identify their desired shoe-type and look at different models to find their preference.

It sure gave his staff an easy intro. "Looking for (basketball) shoes?" was their line.

The next questions were easy, too: "How often do you play?" The answer afforded enough information in their quest to select the right shoe.

Sales went through the roof. (Funny how they all do that now.)

Where are we going with this?

What I want you to do is look closely at what you're doing and ask some questions about what you could do better.

By doing it just 10% or even 5% better, your result would be significant. By increasing your conversion rate by 5% and increasing the spend (like Katie did and, I repeat, as McDonald's do with their famous, "Did you want fries with that?" line) and by selling to them once more every year, your turnover will sky rocket.

If your average is to convert 1000 people per month with an average sale value of $100, adding 5% to each increases your turnover by $5,000 per month. If they buy five times per year and you can raise that to six, you will see another significant increase.

Now imagine that each customer is bringing you one new client per year (through a loyalty program or an affiliate link on the internet) and each one of them does the same thing, your figures and profits will have gone ballistic!

I'm no mathematician but I'm sure I can leave you to do the numbers.

Remember

Know your cost of client acquisition.

Take the time to explain it to your staff.

Chapter 17

The Eight Deadly Sales Sins – What They Are and How to Avoid Them

In bullet point format, here are eight unforgivable sins committed by people in trying to gain and maintain customers. Etch them into your memory.

1. Looking for a "quick fix" to close more sales

Sales are not closed: they're opened.

Solution: You must learn how to open the sale, how to build rapport with your prospective customers and how to develop an understanding of their business or of their lifestyle first.

Only when you have some understanding of from where they're coming can you even hope to advocate a solution in which they'll be interested.

2. Deceptive prospecting/marketing tactics

Don't deceive people with your advertising or prospecting message.

Solution: Before you call a potential new buyer, consider what the reaction to your call might be. Better still, turn it around and ask yourself how *you* would react if you were called with this message.

People are busy today, so calling to ask if you can drop by for a chat or to talk about a mystery is pointless.

Why should people give up their time unless they believe you can do something for them? This is called, *"Intrusion Marketing"* and is generally resented.

3. Not correctly identifying prospects

Don't bother selling to folk who don't need what you sell.

Solution: Develop a buyer profile. Know who is likely to want what you sell and what their buying process is. Identify the key person or people and look to provide answers to their wants and needs. If you can't reach the key person, whomever you can reach has to become your ally or advocate.

Talk in their terms!

4. Focusing on the product not the customer

Let me emphasize again, what they're buying is the sizzle not the sausage.

Solution: Learn to talk about benefits and what they will do to ease pain or solve their problem. Talk about how it will make or save them money. To do this you must be able to relate how each aspect of everything you sell benefits the customer. If people quickly grasp the idea and benefits of your business, it is considered to be infectious. As I have already said, do people nod knowingly as you describe your company's products or services, or do they look puzzled and quickly excuse themselves? If it's the latter, you're not selling benefits.

5. Talking, not listening

How can you listen when you are talking?

Solution: You must learn to ask questions. Use open, closed and, "Tell-me-about" questions to gather information and look for pain! Otherwise, you are trying to "convince". Who wants to be convinced? Essentially, when you do this you are getting into a struggle with the customer, one which you'll never win.

6. Ignoring the customer once the sale is made

Forgetting service, and back-end business opportunities. (Let me repeat, back-end business is generated from a client after you have made the first sale to them.)

Solution: You must understand the lifetime value of a customer.

7. Ignoring testimonials and referrals

In other words, always using cold prospecting techniques to find new clients.

Solution: Develop "warm" enquiries and leads. New business can come from a variety of sources:
- Cold calls.
- Advertising including Direct-Mail and the internet.
- Loose reference groups like the school P&F, family, friends.
- Tight reference groups such as referral clubs and business associations.
- Develop a referral strategy for your business such as, 'get one free after paying for five.' Offer customers entry into prize draws for referrals. I heard of a hairdresser who buys you dinner at the Hilton for introducing just five new clients.

8. Vendor apathy

Vendor apathy is when the supplier doesn't care. It's when your staff don't understand that gaining and maintaining customers is everyone's job.

When a potential buyer calls but you don't call back.

Solution: Create and maintain a "customer first" culture in your business. Teach your staff the absolute importance of each prospect. Teach them how much it costs to open the doors and to advertise. Most don't know. It's just a job...

Explain just how important the customer-focus attitude really is. Provide them with a reason; an incentive based on retention.

Let me make another relevant observation. I frequently see businesses spend huge sums of money on marketing: brochures, adverts, direct mail etc., because their belief is that if they increase their enquiry rate, they will make more sales.

That's only valid if their salespeople can convert those enquiries into business.

Before you spend money on marketing in the attempt to gain more sales, consider how many sales opportunities you'll miss if your staff can't convert the extra leads. Wouldn't you be better to invest in some quality training to improve your conversion rate?

Someone once asked me, "Why would I spend time training my staff only to have them up and leave to work somewhere else?"

I replied, "Why take the risk of not training them and have them stay?"

Remember

It may be your apathy, or the apathy of those around you that is costing you sales.

Chapter 18

How to Increase Your Personal Effectiveness

By now, we've reviewed the main techniques and methods you use when selling. Now we need to examine some of your personal habits.

Let me begin by telling you a story about a salesperson (I'll call him, 'Tony') who once worked for me *(for a very short time I might add. You'll see why soon!)*

Tony interviewed well. He was working for my competitor at the time, and said he'd bring customers with him. He also said he was unhappy there and wanted to leave. Of course, it was hard to call my competitor to reference-check him.

He had all the right answers and looked the part, so I hired him, but soon regretted my decision. His figures were not very encouraging, and what made it worse, he knew all the stuff. However, his call reports showed me that his time effectiveness was very poor. I asked him to more accurately detail how he occupied his day.

Monday morning was spent in my weekly meeting (that was OK, but it finished at 10am) and he was still in the office at 12! He told me he was writing quotes and making appointments. At 12 it was time for lunch, and at 1pm it was time to go out on calls.

His working territory was about half an hour away, so he got there shortly before 2. But his appointment was always at the other side of the territory, so that meant after 2pm. Of course, as it was an industrial area, he reasoned he couldn't see anyone else that day as they all, "knocked off" at 3:30pm, so he went home after his one call.

Tuesday saw him on the road early, but again with badly planned calls, taking him in a criss-cross motion across his territory. He would be back at the office by lunchtime, with a story that he had to talk with the service manager about a customer problem. By then of course, it was too late to go back to his territory.

This story went on day after day. Despite my best efforts to have him change his habits, nothing ever happened. He was spending **less than two hours a day with customers**. Out of an eight-hour working day, less that 25% of his time was being used effectively.

The only activities that our organisation required Tony to participate in that would take him from his customers were a weekly Monday morning sales meeting and a monthly Friday afternoon meeting. Eight hours from every month, yet he could only manage two hours each day to be with customers.

Sadly, we parted company with Tony. A nice guy, and when he worked, a good salesperson. He didn't once meet his quotas though and wouldn't follow our instructions about time and personal management.

We all have time issues. We all need to travel, go to the dentist; we all need time off for illness and holidays. But we all have a profit responsibility.

As an employer, you buy staff time at wholesale price and make a profit from it. In return, employees are required to make sales, attend meetings, and respond to directives and policies. If they fail to do so, they don't deserve their jobs. It's a simple proposition.

If we're self-employed either as a business owner, or as a commission-only salesperson, we must do the time and get the results.

This is one of the prime reasons why employers choose to pay salespeople on a, "fee only" basis. Because they know just how easy it is for people to become like Tony; to have all the skills, but to get no results.

I don't know your industry, your geographic uniqueness or your business. But I do know that each factor is individually unique. That's why I can't tell you what to do each and every day. I can give you a plan to follow, however, and a guide to its implementation.

Here's how we go about it. I want you to take a typical week and divide it into ten sections. These are each half-day from Monday to Friday, between 8am and 12noon, and between 12noon and 5pm.

Start by heading the first page with next week's dates. Then, write any fixed appointments and meetings you have into the blank spaces. The time left is the opportunity-time you have available.

Ask yourself if you have scheduled the meetings and appointments at the most suitable times? Are you travelling unnecessarily between calls? Look to rearrange anything that can give you more time.

Now pencil in a block of time during which you will participate in a prospecting activity. It doesn't matter if its phone-calling, or doorknocking. What you must do is monitor how many of them you do or make. Then write down how many of them are effective (measured by the number of appointments you get) and record the result on the second template.

Monitor the appointment times you make, too, as they will form a pattern you can follow. Vary the time block you use in which to make these calls, and over the ten weeks, you see a pattern that will illustrate the most effective time of the week for you to pursue this activity. Make that time a regular fixed block in your planning system.

Likewise, you will see a pattern of the most suitable times for you to have first or second meetings with your clients. Mark those times in your diary and don't use them for other activities. Keep them free for first and second meetings.

Next, find those times of the week when very little seems to happen. Use those times for the non-productive activities like banking, bookwork, and so on. These activities are necessary and important, but remember the question I asked earlier: "Is what I'm about to do the most productive thing I can do at this moment?"

You should now have your planning templates 75% filled with activities planned at their most suitable time.

The remaining 25% of the time slots are for those unexpected activities - like the new customer enquiries your dynamic lead-generation and referral processes are delivering.

Like the, "Let's proceed" appointment we talked about before, and time for you to take an occasional long lunch.

The strategy focus is to always do things that ruthlessly advance you to your goal.

The tactics, or the doing aspects, are the things you delegate.

Chances are that your competitors aren't tactical; they're just into doing.

If that's the case, you're ahead of them already and by consistently following the strategic issues, you'll stay ahead.

Allow me again to quote Jay Abraham:

"You are the one that has consciously made the decision to do this. It's your choice if you have a crumbling edifice that drains you morally, physically, emotionally and financially, that you have to prop up and that you can't eventually sell."

My question to you is this:

Are you working on stuff you're not good at? Are you using your time for the best possible outcome?

Think back to the commentary in Chapter 2 about your role being to focus on marketing and innovation. They're the strategic issues that generate customers and cash flow.

I was watching a Current Affairs show recently.

The story was about how much time small business owners were spending on government red tape, the filling out of forms and reports. A café owner was interviewed, and his story illustrates my point. Here's the gist of his commentary...

He got involved in the café because he enjoyed the industry and was in fact, a very good frontman. His problem was that he was spending far too many hours drowning in paperwork instead of fronting the café.

My slant is this; if he's the best person to be doing the customer, meet-and-greet or the best person at selling and up-selling, why doesn't he delegate the paperwork?

My guess is that he doesn't value his time. Surely he can create more profit by delegating the bookwork than by doing it himself?

In his classic book, *The E-Myth*, Michael Gerber talks about working on your business, not in your business.

Even if you *are* the business, you owe it to yourself to spend time working on its strategy, planning and systemisation.

Prioritise the Important over the Urgent by remembering that someone else's Urgent is just that: someone else's.

Identify the most important tasks that you must do each day, then tackle them in priority one-by-one. Learn to say, "No" to interruptions. Put your phone onto voicemail occasionally. Undo the umbilical cord between you and the cell phone. Ignore emails for a few hours.

What I'm encouraging you to do is to take stock of your current situation, and to look for a better view of it. Create a better vision for yourself and set out to achieve it. Do it now, not tomorrow, not next week.

One way to begin is to write a few little lists, each that starts with a description of the thing you don't want. Follow it with what you do want in its place. Describe how it looks and feels.

Now, imagine you're there having achieved that goal. Turn around and walk back down the road you've travelled to reach that destination. Write down the events that happened at each step until you're back where you are today.

Reverse the order and you have a track for achieving your goal. Now walk it again, this time knowing where you're heading and how you're going to get there.

The stumbling blocks along the way represent the areas where you need help. Go get that help now instead of when you get to the block. That way, your track will be clear and there's no excuse!

Remember

You don't know what you don't know - *until you know it!*

Chapter 19

About the Deviation

At the start, I told you about Rex and selling home security systems...

You will recall that we were on the third appointment for the night and things weren't looking good for Rex. I had interrupted his presentation by insisting we go out to the car.

"What's this all about?" Rex demanded as we retrieved the demo system. "I was on a roll back there."

"No you weren't," I replied. "You're dead in the water but you can salvage it. When we go back inside, sit where I was sitting and look to your right at what's on the wall behind the bar."

What I haven't told you is that Rex was an apprentice jockey and that behind the bar were several photos of racehorses passing the winning post.

We went back inside, and Rex saw the photos.

"Oh wow, is that your horse" he asked, pointing at one of the pictures.

"They're all ours," the husband replied. "Why?"

Pointing at another picture, Rex replied, "I rode that one this morning, I'm apprenticed to your trainer!"

I'm not into horses or horse racing and the next hour was for me about as exciting as watching paint dry. Their conversation was enthusiastic, animated, and very friendly. Rex had done something new; he had started to build trust and develop a relationship.

It was getting late, maybe close to 10pm when the front door opened and in came their daughter and son-in-law returning home from dinner.

We were introduced to the family and the wife said she would go and make tea for us all. As she walked into the kitchen, she turned to her husband and told him to get their cheque book and write a cheque for two systems, one for them and one for their daughter's house.

Rex went back to the office the next morning – suddenly a hero for selling two alarms on one call. He phoned me a month later to say he never used the script verbatim again - and to tell me he'd topped the sales charts for the last three weeks.

Rex recognised that the sales process has constant context, but the content changes every time.

Conclusion

Learning to sell is not an instant process; improvement will take you weeks or even months. Nothing worthwhile happens overnight; especially this. It takes commitment. I can only provide you with the processes; I can't make you apply them.

You owe it to yourself to test, change and monitor your performance for the better.

Why settle for a methodology that brings you only part of what you deserve?

One phrase you change, one headline you adjust, one varied question that you ask can make the difference between a mediocre result and an awesome result.

What are you waiting for?

Put the book down and go sell something...
James

From The Lighter Side of Selling

The Sales Manager's Thesaurus

When the buyer says...	What they mean is...	What the salesperson reported...
I'll think about it	I haven't time to give you an answer now	Buyer is discussing our proposition with his boss
I'm still thinking about it	I haven't even thought about it	Our proposition is receiving significant consideration
We haven't decided yet	Still haven't thought about it	Proposal is still under consideration
We're looking around	Your deal isn't good enough	The proposal under consideration along with others
Call me next week	Go away for a while	Decision imminent. Call next week for order
Call me in two weeks	He might forget to call	Decision imminent. Call in two weeks for an order
Call me next month / two months / six months	GO AWAY!!!	Decision delayed. I will keep in touch.
We need to talk with our Accountant	He's tough enough to say no, so I don't have to	The proposal is under finance consideration. Call again next week.
To be put to the Board for approval	I haven't got the authority to say yes, and I don't think they will approve it anyway	Senior management expressed significant interest in our proposal. Tabled for discussion at next Board meeting.

You're too expensive	My mate Fred says he'll beat any price you submit, so go away	We need to review our pricing as our competitor is cheaper than us all the time
We've selected your competitor's offer	We liked him more, and he took us to a nicer place for lunch	Decided to trial competitors' products before sampling ours
No	No	Buyer too busy to talk with me
Have a long-term contract with your competitor	Don't show your face here again, you lying SOB	I can't sell to him. He's too hard.

The Buyers Thesaurus

What the salesperson said...	What the salesperson meant...
We're having a special this week	I haven't met my quota this month, and I'm desperate
I can get you extended credit	I want the figures for my chart to look good this month.
They won't last at this price	We couldn't sell any at a higher price
We have a few left in stock	We haven't sold any yet
Attractively priced	Boss is desperate to quit them
New model coming	Boss won't stock the new one until we've sold this old stuff.
I can't hold this price	Wait ten days, and they'll be cheaper.

forever.	
No, we don't have any real competition	Don't you read the trade magazines? Their name is everywhere!
I may be able to do you a better price.	Why should I offer you my best price upfront? You might just have bought at full price, and I'd make more commission.
If you buy in larger quantities, I'll give you a better price	That way, I don't have to come all the way out here to see you as often
Of course, we can deliver!	I hope I can get one in by then.
Yes, we can do onsite service	That's if I can ever get that lazy technician of ours to get off his butt and get out here
Would you like tickets to see the football from our box on Sunday?	If wasting my Sunday with you is the only way I can get your money, so be it.
What about we have lunch?	Hopefully, you'll get drunk and say yes to my proposal.
OK, I'll ask my boss if we can do that for you	I don't want to look like I'm the one who's ripping you off

I apologise to all of the great clients and the wonderful salespeople I've worked with and dealt with over the last 30 + years!

About The Author

It has been said more than once that James Yuille has sales and marketing in his DNA!

James is a 40-plus-year sales and marketing veteran. His career started in Adelaide, South Australia, where, in 12 months, he sold office equipment and cold-called every commercial premise in Adelaide.

At the age of 21, in a demanding sales job, he created a sales system called TIPS, which changed how his employer sold their products and made him their top salesperson in his first year in sales.

Over the next 15 years, he set new sales records in every company he worked for. In one three-month period in 1991, he sold over $1,000,000 of facsimile machines worth $3,000 each.

As the state sales manager for a Japanese multinational company, he grew the division from one person (himself) to a team of 15.

In 1999, he saw the marketing potential of the Internet and built an optimised website that increased the company's revenue by over $100,000 that year.

In 2000, he opened a marketing consultancy business that sold websites, graphic design, copywriting, and sales training. In 2002, when Google released their AdWords, James saw the potential and started building campaigns to help clients generate more leads.

Since then, he has created and managed hundreds of accounts for a diverse range of clients, from baby clothing to funeral directors, construction, home improvement, consulting, and finance.

Over the years, James generated hundreds of millions of dollars in sales for his clients, one of whom, at the start-up stage in 2001, has grown to be a multinational employing 70 staff with an annual turnover of over $25,000,000. That business sold in 2001 for close to a billion dollars.

Today, James runs Mediaglue, a digital marketing business focused on helping clients grow their businesses through effective marketing and sales processes.